The Party's Over . . .

Living Without Leah

The Party's Over . . .
Living without Leah

Janet and Paul Betts
with Ivan Sage

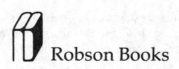

Robson Books

First published in Great Britain in 1997 by Robson
Books Ltd, Bolsover House, 5–6 Clipstone Street,
London W1P 8LE

British Library Cataloguing in Publication Data
A catalogue record for this title is available from the
British Library

ISBN 1 86105 116 6

Photoset in North Wales by Derek Doyle & Associates,
Mold, Flintshire. Printed in Great Britain by Butler &
Tanner Ltd, London and Frome.

In Memory of Leah

God grant me the serenity to accept the things I cannot change;
the courage to change the things I can;
and the wisdom to know the difference.

Contents

Introduction

'When people take drugs it only affects their bodies, doesn't it?
But when they become ill or die it affects everyone.'
Leah Betts' 11-year-old half-brother William

OK, so you've just picked up this book and opened it to see if it has
something to offer you. You have just taken the first step in what, I
hope, will be a learning experience. You would have had to have
been on another planet not to have heard at least something about
the fate that befell young Leah Betts, the teenager who fell victim
to an Ecstasy tablet and who has since become an icon in the war
against drugs.

To dismiss what happened to Leah – to pretend it could never
happen to you, or one of your family or friends – is to bury your
head in the sand. If you really believe that what happened to her
was a one-off, a freakish accident, then this book is not for you.
However, if you are at least open-minded enough to accept the
possibility that it could happen again – as indeed it has, many times
over – please read on.

Without doubt, Leah's father Paul, and stepmother Janet are the
bravest couple I have ever met. I will never forget my first meeting
with them. It was on November 1 1996, Leah's 19th birthday – or,
at least, it should have been. Leah had died just under a year previously, at her belated 18th birthday party. She had taken just one
Ecstasy tablet but that had been enough to kill her. Her death made

headline news, not just throughout the United Kingdom, but internationally, as a result of Paul and Janet's decision to release a photograph of their daughter connected to a life-support machine.

Twelve months later, through my work as a reporter on a local newspaper, I contacted Paul and Janet with the intention of producing a feature on how Leah's death had affected their lives. Leah's party had taken place on November 11 the previous year which, I assumed, had been the date of her birthday. But when I arrived at the Betts' cottage in rural Essex, I discovered it would have been Leah's birthday that very day. In the corner of the room, on top of the television set, stood a photograph of Leah. Poignantly, standing next to it, was a burning candle.

Under the circumstances, I was surprised Paul and Janet were prepared to speak to anyone from the press that day. It had obviously been a difficult day for them both, and I offered to come back another time. However, they were adamant we should carry on as arranged, such was their determination to put across their message about the dangers of drug abuse.

During the course of the interview there were times when the recollections of that fateful night proved too much for Paul, the painful memories moving him to tears. When I had completed the interview, I headed homewards with very mixed emotions. I knew I could produce a good feature from the information Paul and Janet had passed on to me. I also knew this would be one of the most moving articles I had ever written. On the other hand, the sight of Paul with tears in his eyes and Janet's loving gestures to comfort him had created a lump in my throat that felt the size of a football.

Their efforts to highlight what had happened to their daughter in order to educate other youngsters and their parents filled me with admiration. They had worked tirelessly over that year – and have done ever since – to promote their drugs-awareness campaign and they were determined to do everything in their power to prevent a similar tragedy happening again.

A few nights later I revisited Paul and Janet to show them the completed feature. Janet was impressed. Paul, however, could not bear to read it. It was impossible not to be moved.

I feel very privileged to have been asked by Paul and Janet to help them produce this book as they continue their crusade against the drug culture that is so prevalent in our society. This is the story of a family fighting back from a wasteful, needless death. Neither Paul nor Janet had any idea that Leah had ever taken Ecstasy before or, for that matter, any other substance.

Their message will, hopefully, be powerful enough to make other youngsters who read it think twice before making the same choice as Leah. Hopefully, it will also make parents more aware of the warning signs of drug abuse. To any parent who insists that such a fate could never happen to one of their own, I can only say – think again! How well do we really know our own children or who they associate with?

Thanks to Paul and Janet, the issue of so-called 'recreational' drugs is one many youngsters and parents are now more aware of. It is so easy to assume our own children would never experiment with drugs, but how can we really be so sure?

The complacency shown by some people is deeply worrying. We should talk to our children and show them the photograph in this book of Leah connected to the life-support machine to leave them in no doubt about the agony Ecstasy and other drugs can cause.

There are no guarantees that any amount of education will dissuade someone from taking drugs but, as individuals and as parents, we have a responsibility to do everything we can to make ourselves fully aware of the potential dangers faced if tempted to experiment.

A drug user is, perhaps unconsciously, a selfish person. Although that person may be willing to gamble his or her health, or life, in their search for momentary pleasure, it is very unlikely they have stopped to consider the catastrophic effects their actions may have, not only on themselves, but on their family and friends.

Anyone who believes the drug pusher they might meet on a street corner or in a night club really gives a damn if they have a good night on Ecstasy, or any other substance he may be able to peddle, is living in cloud-cuckoo land. All he is really interested in is lining his own pockets. How can anyone be sure what they are taking?

The drug culture has become a cancer in our society. Those who oppose it are often subjected to scorn, ridicule or threats. But that does not mean this is a problem that should not be tackled head-on.

People like Paul and Janet deserve our utmost admiration for the way they have battled, against all the odds, to raise awareness.

I challenge any reader not to be deeply moved by their story. They have turned Leah's death into something positive, something of value. I hope their message will hit home to every parent and youngster who reads this book. That, I believe, would be the most fitting tribute to their determination.

IVAN SAGE

Prologue

JANET: Standing at the third floor window, staring at the lights of the M25 and the town in between, I was on the point of making yet another cup of tea, bang in the middle of yet another night duty. It was very quiet on the ward – only eight patients, all of whom were self-caring, as was often the case on a Bank Holiday weekend, and I had just finished a tour of all the occupied beds.

All was well, everyone warm and sound asleep, which was more than could be said for me. I was frozen, partly because I was tired. The day room was warmer, and a good place to take stock and think, as well as get warm. Then I heard the lift ascending. Out bounced one of my colleagues. I remember thinking how I wished I was twenty-something again and could have that much energy at three in the morning! She apparently had felt thoroughly 'uncomfortable' with her boyfriend of that evening, and just walked to the hospital for a chat.

She talked nineteen to the dozen, hardly pausing for breath, while walking around and around the day room. She looked very pretty, especially her eyes, although her long hair was hanging in lank strands as though she had been caught in the rain. I commented on the fact and she grinned.

After about an hour, she disappeared as suddenly as she arrived, to walk home to shower and change ready for the early shift. At 7 am she turned up on the ward, looking somewhat depressed. I told her to cheer up, and commented it must have been the lack of sleep!

'I don't know how she does it,' I commented to another colleague several nights later. 'I can remember when my girls were little, going to a party and putting them to bed upstairs at our friends' house, then having to get up at six the following morning with them, but I looked and felt like a dead duck!' I put it down to middle age. There was a veil between her social life, culture and me. She was only two years older than my eldest daughter, and we had a good rapport. We discussed everything.

But I was naïve and uneducated. I was a parent.

We have written this book because we felt we had to – for ourselves but, most of all, to Leah's memory. The hurt of losing a child is indescribable. Those who have been through the experience will know what we mean. Those of you who have lost, or nearly lost, a child in similar circumstances will understand why we cannot let any of the experiences we have been through, or any of the knowledge gained, be forgotten. We invite you to share our learning experience.

1

Early Days

JANET: We were sitting in the kitchen when, suddenly, our 11-year-old son William came running downstairs.

'Mum, Leah needs you, she's not well...'

It was November 11 1995, on the occasion of Leah's 18th birthday party, and our home was full of teenagers enjoying the happy atmosphere. But, when we went upstairs to Leah, the ambience was shattered as, within minutes, our beautiful daughter was lying lifelessly, cradled in her father's arms. And so began a sequence of events that saw our family catapulted from relative obscurity to the front pages of the national press and television news programmes, the result of our decision to go public about the circumstances of Leah's death.

We realise many who have read or heard about Leah's death from taking an Ecstasy tablet can only see the issue of a young druggie whose luck ran out. In order to correct that misconception, it is necessary to give an insight into Leah's life and that of our family. Only then will those people realise that, prior to her death, Leah was just an ordinary girl from an ordinary family. Only then will readers perhaps come to the conclusion, 'There, but for the grace of God, go I.'

PAUL: I was such a proud father when Dorothy – or Dot as she was known in the family – gave birth to Leah on November 1 1977 in

Romford, Essex. Dorothy was a school teacher at Campbell School in nearby Dagenham. We had married five years previously. I was a former teacher myself but, by the time Leah came along, I was a sergeant in the police force, a career familiar to Dot as her father had also served in the force. After a honeymoon in Alderney, we set up home in police accommodation in Forest Gate, London.

I had been on night duty at Leytonstone police station. Dot was having a very hard labour and Leah was in no hurry to enter the world, eventually being born in the early evening. I was at her birth. During the period of labour, I was encouraging Dot by giving her a running commentary, which I now realise she didn't fully appreciate at the time! As Leah was delivered, the cord was around her neck, but otherwise everything seemed to go normally. I was so proud. What a brilliant experience!

It's funny, isn't it – we are trained for everything in life except parenthood, and at first, whenever Leah started to cry at night (which was often) we would pick her up to settle her. Sometimes I could hardly keep my eyes open as I rocked her carrycot.

Leah had a good pair of lungs on her, she could really scream. Eventually it got to a stage when we realised that she would cry herself to sleep if we just left her to it. After that, we didn't have a problem. When she was a little girl, I used to help her to sleep each night by reading the Red Hen, Henny Penny stories. Leah really loved it when I read to her.

Unfortunately, in 1979, I suffered from meningitis and, at about the same time, our marriage was starting to run into difficulty. Dot was a very career-minded woman and, rightly or wrongly, I felt her main interest in life was her work. She was a very good teacher but I believed her ambition to become a headmistress overrode her family commitments. As a result, I began to feel very lonely and our marriage just went downhill.

I must accept my share of the blame for the break-up but it was a very difficult time. In 1982, when Leah was just four years old, Dot and I were divorced. After that, my time with Leah was limited to one weekend a fortnight and I was not permitted to take her on holidays with me. I was so afraid that Leah and I would drift apart but, fortunately, she always wanted to come to see me. In fact, when she became a teenager, she began to visit on a much more regular basis.

Prior to our divorce, Dot and I were often invited to parties, or would go on fishing trips, with two friends, Alec and Jan Lambert. Alec was a policeman who worked with me at the station and we were very good friends. The first time I met Jan, his wife, was on our return from a fishing trip. She was painting the front room of their house with a friend in Dagenham. Although she was only wearing a tatty old pair of trousers, something tied around her head and had paint smudges all over her, I couldn't help thinking how lucky Alec was to have such a lovely wife.

My envy was no doubt due to the difficulties in my own marriage at the time. It wasn't long before I discovered Jan and Alec's marriage was also in difficulty. As a result, I think Jan and I found we could empathise with each other, and empathy can be a very powerful and attractive feeling.

JANET: I began my nursing career training as a cadet at Rush Green Hospital, near Romford, when I was 16 years old but, after eight months, I went back to college and then to work for May & Baker in the medicinal organic chemistry department. When I think back now, some of those medicines were revolutionary. Now they are just taken for granted. I met Alec at college and we married in 1971. We had three daughters: Wendy, our first, was born in 1973, Emily followed in 1975 and Cindy in 1976. We lived near the Ford motor works in Dagenham. Alec joined the police force in 1972 where he worked under Paul. We divorced in 1981

When Paul and I started to go out together, Leah was hardly a stranger to me. Alec and I had often gone out as a foursome with Paul and Dot, so I had known Leah since she was a baby. She was a cute little thing. My most vivid early memories of her are when she was a baby in a yellow fluffy one-piece suit and as a toddler in her little red wellies.

When she was about eight months old she suffered badly from eczema. She also suffered from asthma until about the age of seven.

She loved being told stories. She was the original little cute kid. I used to sit her on my lap whenever we were together and I would tell her the story of Cinderella, like my father used to tell it to me. When it got to the part where Cinderella wanted to go to the ball – 'What you? ... YOU go to the ball ???!!!' – I would prod her tummy and she would scream with laughter.

PAUL: Jan and I found that we got on really well and both felt that our partners did not really care about us. I suppose that's what led to the gates being opened. We met again at a policewoman friend's wedding. By now I was on my own and Jan was separated from Alec. When the wedding vows were being exchanged, I turned and saw Jan and something just clicked. I asked her out for a drink the next day and one thing led to another. Dot divorced me for adultery, which I never challenged, and I then left the matrimonial home.

I left everything to Dot. Money was tight, as I was paying two mortgages, but the hardest thing I had ever had to do at the time was to leave Leah behind. She was only three years old when I left home but she didn't understand what was going on. Dorothy had a lot of hate for me after the divorce and, at one stage, I suppose Leah became the subject of an emotional tug-of-war between her mother and me. I regret it now.

I tried to put the record straight with Leah when she was older, but she believed in her mum and I had sufficient respect for her not to burst her bubble. The whole thing was like a bombshell to Leah a few years later when she began to understand more and ask more questions. It was as if her whole world had collapsed. All I can say is that, when I'm put in my box, I'll be taking the truth of what happened with me.

Not long after I left home Dot's new partner, Chris, moved in with her. They soon sold up and moved, with Leah, to Laindon, near Basildon. Jan and I started to live together at Jan's place in Dagenham. After a while, we decided we wanted to get married. We are both Christians and we believed God wanted us to be happy together, rather than live unhappily with someone we no longer loved.

Unfortunately, the church would not entertain marrying divorcees. However, there was a Methodist church not far from us and we asked the minister if he would allow us to marry. He was quite happy to conduct the ceremony. And so, on September 25, 1982, Jan and I were married. We were strapped for cash at the time, so our friends did the catering. The only things we bought were Jan's wedding dress and four dresses for the girls.

JANET: Because Dot was a teacher, Leah could read from a very early age. She was quite knowledgeable and used to go into school with her mother during her primary school years. After Paul and I began to live together, Leah used to love to come over to see my girls. I can honestly say, hand on heart, that there were no problems with Leah getting used to having three step-sisters. After all, she had known them all as friends since she was a baby. In fact, all four girls were bridesmaids when Paul and I were married.

Leah joined the Brownies and became a majorette. From the age of five years until she was about ten, she used to love dressing up with the other girls to do a party piece with them. We have many videos of those happy times to look back on.

It wasn't until her secondary school years that Leah transferred to a school in Basildon. She was a very studious pupil, always very bright, always smiling and willing to help her friends. We used to work together on her English literature homework, going through extracts of Shakespeare line by line.

She always wanted to learn and hoped to become a teacher, like her mother, when she finished her studies. She was quite capable of doing so, having gained eight GCSEs. While at Basildon College Leah studied biology, chemistry and psychology. Dot would have been a very hard act to follow, career-wise. She was a very well respected teacher who had risen to the position of assistant head-mistress.

Leah was a very happy child and we got on really well. She became such a good friend to me. I don't recall having an argument with her at all, although I sometimes had to smooth over tiffs she had with Paul, as you might expect with any teenage daughter.

Looking back to when she was younger, Leah had quite a job understanding the value of money. At first she found it difficult to understand why, at Christmas, we had five children to buy for as compared with being the centre of attention when Paul and Dot were together.

I don't think Leah ever felt torn between her mother and me. Her mother was her mother ... end of story. She called me mum but I never attempted to take Dot's place.

PAUL: In 1992, Dot became very ill. On September 1 she collapsed. When Leah and Chris found her they tried artificial respiration and got her to hospital, but she was dead on arrival. She was only 45. Leah took the death of her mother very badly. At her age – she was 14 years old by now – she was missing me, and although she had all she seemed to need in a material sense, she still harboured hopes that her mum and I would eventually get back together, even though I had married Jan.

Dot's death made my access to Leah easier. That may seem a callous thing to say but, as many divorced fathers discover, there are often problems when it comes to arranging access to the children. Leah no longer had to endure that old 'tug-of-war' and, for the first time in many years, I had my daughter back.

Any family that claims they never have a cross word are liars, but Leah and I enjoyed a very close relationship even though we sometimes fought like cat and dog! What I liked most of all about her was her straight talking. She was like me. We could usually come to an agreement eventually, but, because of puberty, boyfriends and everything else, I could happily have strangled her sometimes. In spite of all that, we had such a lot of love for each other.

On April 12, 1984 our family expanded when Jan gave birth to our son William. Leah and the other girls loved him and found having a baby in the house quite a novelty. They all loved to feed and bath him and do everything for him. However, when he grew up enough to wander around and answer them back or interrupt them, that's when the blood-curdling cries and banshee wailing began between them! Although they loved him, the girls were now growing up and they didn't consider it to be the 'in' thing to allow a little brother to be part and parcel of all the goings on when friends came around. Still, whenever he really needed any of the girls, they were always there for him.

Leah had a good rapport with Jan's girls, especially Wendy, who became her confidant. She also enjoyed Emily's company. If ever there was to be a spat, it was usually between Leah and Cindy, although they too, usually got on extremely well with each other. With William, it was usually the big sister to little brother relationship. Sometimes Leah couldn't get enough of him, other times she just wanted him to go away. Nevertheless, she really loved him. He was after all, her very own brother.

As for boyfriends, the only one we met was a really nice young lad called Lee, who thought the world of Leah. They were both about 16 years old at the time. There were other casual boyfriends later on but we didn't know them. Leah's best friend was Sarah Cargill, who went to the same school and, later, college in Basildon. Those two were inseparable. Sarah was to feature largely in later years for reasons that will become clear as this story unfolds.

Leah was a bubbly, extrovert person – rather like me, according to Jan! But, if she got an idea in her head that you didn't agree with, God help you! However, once she calmed down, you could at least talk things through with her reasonably and, in her defence, she was never one for sulking. She was not what you might call a difficult kid. In fact, when my mother was alive and living with us, Leah was very good to her.

Many years ago I was the chairman of an organisation called the Friends of Yew Tree Lodge, a hostel for the disabled in Romford. We used to raise money for the residents. One of our projects was to raise money for a mini-bus and Leah was quite happy to wear a silly hat to go along to Romford Carnival to help raise money for the cause. She was very good with disabled people. She could accept people's disabilities. Many people, when they meet someone in a wheelchair, talk to the person pushing it rather than the person sitting in it. I think it's called the 'Does he take sugar?' syndrome. Leah was never like that.

Discipline was never a real problem with Leah. Usually a raised voice would do the trick. It may sound selfish but my motto has always been, 'My kids live with me, not me with them.' I can never remember having smacked Leah but I often recall having wagged my finger at her! Until the last three years of Leah's life, I had not had much involvement in her upbringing and I think I then may have become over-protective. It was quite an eye-opener. I never really thought I would be like that.

Leah was a typical teenage girl. She was an avid Oasis fan: 'Wonderwall' was the morning, noon and night record. The walls vibrated to the music! She was boots and shoes mad and was always buying them. She was into foreign travel and languages and spoke very good French. She often went to France with her mother and was considering spending a year there before starting at university.

Although she was such a music fan, she was not always going to nightclubs or discotheques and was quite happy just to stay at home with us, even though she had a wide range of friends. She loved to go sailing and swimming – until she discovered boys!

Because money had always been hard to come by after my divorce, we used to take her out on our small yacht for sailing holidays or go camping. But, when she was 17, she went on her 'holiday of a lifetime' with Sarah to Benidorm and was planning to go again a year later. To make ends meet while she was at college, Leah worked on the ladies' fashion sales counter at Allders, the big department store in Basildon, on Saturdays.

After all the years we spent apart, the moments I cherished most with Leah were when I was able to put my arms around her, give her a kiss and tell her how much I loved her. She was such a loving person, very tactile. Love ... that's one commodity this family has never been short of. We were, then, an ordinary family, not so different from many others. Little did we realise, in the late autumn of 1995, that pictures of our beloved Leah would soon be splashed across the front pages of newspapers far and wide.

Life for our family would never be the same again.

2

The Party Night

JANET: Like any mum, I have to confess, I was in a complete panic about this party. Leah had asked soon after her 17th birthday if she could have a party for her 18th and had been talking around the idea ever since. Her birthday was actually on November 1, which fell midweek and, as she and her friends were planning to go to a bonfire night party on Saturday the fourth, she decided to keep a date special to her, and make her celebration on the 11th.

I can remember being at work the day before, discussing the pros and cons of having 20 to 30 teenagers in the house for this party. 'At least,' I said to my friend Jean Rollinson, 'we'll know what they're up to!' I had no idea of what was about to happen to our lives.

The cost of the party was a major consideration for us owing to Paul's enforced retirement from the police force. In August 1994, Paul, who was a police inspector at the time, and two other police officers, had been called out to a disturbance at a wedding at St Peter's church in Dagenham. It seems that the bride's mother was not too happy with her daughter's choice of husband and had turned up at the church to cause a scene. The police were called. The officers warned the lady that she would be arrested for a breach of the peace if she did not quieten down. She agreed, so Paul and his colleagues left.

Half an hour later they were called back. It seems the lady hadn't quite got the message. She was warned once more that if she did not leave, she would be arrested. Her answer was 'Let's make it worth it then,' and she swung around suddenly. She was holding a Coke can. The ring-pull struck Paul just above the right eye, sliced the eyebrow and severed the artery and the muscle at the back of his eye.

The impact knocked Paul to the ground. Believe it or not, a Coke can is quite heavy when it hits you with force in the face! He was bleeding badly. Paul's colleagues arrested the woman. Nobody came to Paul's aid.

Meanwhile, the woman's son tried to stop her arrest, so Paul wrestled him to the ground. Suddenly, Paul realised that he had been surrounded by 15 or so yobs, chanting 'We're gonna kick your f***ing head in' and other obscenities. In Paul's own words, 'I had never been so scared in all my life'. Nevertheless, he continued to hang on to the woman's son, who was eventually arrested.

Paul was taken to hospital to be treated for his injuries. That was the end of his career in the police force. His injuries sustained that day mean he will progressively lose the sight of his right eye, but the official reason for his leaving the force was given as Post-Traumatic Stress Syndrome – or, as Paul says, 'I just lost my bottle'. He just couldn't face the prospect of another situation like that.

As a result, Paul lost two and a half years' earnings. He was deemed unfit to work because of his injuries. He is now on a police pension and we have had to make do with that and my income as a school nurse. The woman, by the way, was ordered to pay Paul damages of £500, payable at £10 a week. So much for British justice!

Paul never received any criminal compensation for the injury that ended his career and, because he has frequently appeared on television since Leah's death to talk about drugs awareness, the little extra payment he had been receiving on his pension was terminated because, he was told, he could 'no longer be suffering from stress'. How little these so-called professionals understand! Paul always has to rise above his grief to appear on television to get the message across. They don't see him crying when we are alone.

★

We had told Leah that she had a choice between a decent present or a party. She chose the party and we had it in mind to go out the day after the party for a meal at a local pub with Wendy, Cindy, Emily and Sarah.

The possibility that people might bring drugs into the house had never entered our heads. The old-fashioned idea of one drink too many did, however, so we moved our little stash of Christmas sherry, and whisky for 'medicinal purposes', and, knowing they would want to dance in limited space, we cleared the whole room. Our lounge, thus emptied, turned our dining room into what looked like a removal firm's storage warehouse, so the food was laid out in the kitchen.

Paul and I toyed with the idea of going to a rather formal yacht club dinner being held at a country club only two miles away. But, as William was excluded from this, we didn't think the unleashed presence of an 11-year-old at an 18th birthday party would go down too well. We told Leah we would be staying in the house, but out of the way, so as not to 'cramp her style'. She had laughed and said she would rather we were there anyway as our house is in the middle of nowhere.

We spent all day clearing the house, preparing food, and, in my case, moaning constantly, as I felt under the weather that day, wishing it was all over and that I was in bed. For that I shall always feel guilty. Leah had been at her Saturday job that day and, at about 4pm, Paul went to collect her and Sarah from Sarah's house in Basildon. Meanwhile, I plodded on with preparing the food. Leah had chosen her buffet menu and, for some reason, had gone mad on tuna. She had originally wanted around 50 people to come to the party, but we suggested it would be too expensive. We settled for 30 and Leah had invited all her friends from college and elsewhere.

A couple of hours or so before the party was due to begin, Leah was all bubbly and excited and disappeared with Sarah for what seemed an eternity upstairs as they prepared themselves in the bathroom. Then, two or three of Leah's friends rang up to say they wouldn't be able to come for one reason or another. Leah was so upset. She sat on Paul's knee in the kitchen and began to cry. 'No-one's gonna turn up.' Sarah tried to reassure her. 'Don't be so daft, the same thing happened at my party.'

We told Leah that we would only provide Coke or lemonade because some of her friends were under 18. We suggested that if any of her older friends wanted to drink alcohol they should bring their own. We made all the food ourselves, except for the birthday cake. Leah had decided she would like one with candles on it and she wanted to be sung to!

PAUL: At about 8 o'clock that evening Leah came downstairs with her arms in the air. She spun around in the doorway and said: 'Will I do?' She looked absolutely incredible, stunning. If I had been 20 or 30 years younger, I would have fancied her myself. She was wearing dark lipstick, eyeshade, a brushed velvet purple top and a long black pencil skirt. She looked really tasty. All of a sudden I realised my little girl had grown up. It was really quite an eye-opener, quite a shock. *I had no idea that, just 15 minutes previously, Leah and Sarah had each taken an Ecstasy tablet.*

The first guests began to arrive about 8.30pm. They were all very pleasant and all came to see Jan and me throughout the evening as we guarded the food table in the kitchen and watched Whitney Houston in the film *The Bodyguard* on television. Outside, it was a pleasant evening and the front door was wide open. Some of Leah's friends had wandered out into the front garden to get some air and to have a smoke. William came in to us to tell us some people were smoking in the porch and front garden. William hates the smell of cigarettes. We were later to find out some of the youngsters had been smoking cannabis, but we had no idea at the time as we were unable to smell anything from the confines of the kitchen.

There was a lovely atmosphere at the party and, although the music was pretty loud, it didn't matter as our house is in the middle of nowhere so we were not disturbing anyone. There was Oasis, REM, and other groups, plus some more smoochy types of records. There was no running up and downstairs or screaming around. On a couple of occasions I went into the lounge to see how things were going along and everything seemed to be fine.

The first time I did so, Leah grabbed hold of me for a dance. It was one of those arms around the neck, arms around the waist type of dances to the song 'When a Man Loves a Woman'. It was really nice. I think that was one of the closest times, both emotionally and physically, I had ever been to Leah. I thought: 'We've cracked it, after all those years apart, now we're together.'

I had a couple of dances before returning to Jan in the kitchen. I didn't want to cramp Leah's style and besides, I wanted to see the rest of the film. There were still a couple of youngsters smoking in the porch but I could tell they had ordinary cigarettes from the smell. As far as I was concerned, everything was going really well.

It was some time now since Leah had taken the tablet but there was nothing in her behaviour to arouse any suspicions in my mind. In any case, I wasn't looking out for anything like that. That sort of thing didn't happen in our family. We didn't need anything like that, did we? We were just a normal family. That was the biggest mistake I have ever made in my life.

At midnight, we brought in the birthday cake. It was in the shape of the figure 18 and decorated in white and yellow icing with candles on top. We sang to Leah and she blew out the candles. That was when one of our friends took the last photograph of Leah. It was a lovely occasion but, unseen within her, a time bomb was ticking away.

Half an hour later we were still in the kitchen, still watching *The Bodyguard*. The party had quietened down a bit and the food was going well. Suddenly William came diving through the door: 'Mum, Leah needs you, she's not well!'

JANET: I thought, 'Here we go, she's had too much to eat.' I went upstairs and Leah was in the bathroom with her back to me, leaning over the washbasin. When she turned round and looked at me, instantly the nurse in me switched on. I saw her eyes. They were black like eyes in a horror film. There were no irises and her pupils were so dilated. I thought, this is either a head injury or drugs.

Obviously it couldn't have been a head injury as she was standing up. It had to be drugs.

'Leah, what on earth have you been up to?' I asked.

She replied instantly: 'I've taken an Ecstasy tablet.' She was sensible enough to realise she had to tell us what we needed to know if we were to be able to help her. Then she began to collapse in my arms and knelt on the floor over the toilet.

I told William to get Paul because the bathroom was quite small and Leah was getting wrapped around the door. Then she threw an almighty throw-up down the loo and started to tell me her legs were giving way. She had a panicky voice. She was sick again as Paul arrived in the bathroom. Leah was sitting on the floor next to the toilet, with me next to her.

I told Paul about the Ecstasy. He had heard of it but knew nothing about it, other than it was the kind of drug used at a rave.

'If she keeps being sick, perhaps it will wear off,' he said hopefully. But then, Leah's body started to go stiff and she began to twitch. We decided to move her into our bedroom. She was only about eight stone in weight but, in her collapsed state, she seemed much heavier.

We laid her on the bedroom floor at the foot of our bed. Paul put her into the recovery position. She was still conscious and talking to us. Paul reverted to police officer mode and instinctively asked Leah to tell us as much as she could before she lost consciousness. By this time Leah was becoming very distressed and in great pain. She knew well that she was in big trouble.

PAUL: I was consumed by a mixture of anger and fear and was thinking of going downstairs to find the bastard who had given Leah the tablet. Someone had to pay. It had not entered my mind that Leah had taken the tablet because she wanted to. I asked Leah who she had got it from. 'Stephen Smith,' she replied, and adding that this was the fourth or fifth time she had taken Ecstasy. Smith's name meant nothing to us.

Then Leah started to hallucinate. She continued to go rigid and began to scream – an indescribable scream – because of the pains in her head. By this time, Jan had the telephone in her hand. It was time to ring an ambulance. We needed help – and fast.

I was still on the floor with Leah. Jan dialled 99— but, before she had dialled the final 9, Leah stopped breathing. There were just a couple of snores and then – nothing. Jan and I just looked at each other   this simply could not be happening to us!

JANET: I got through to ambulance control. By now Paul was down on the floor starting to try to resuscitate Leah.

'*Ambulance, emergency.*'

'Our daughter's at a party. She's taken Ecstasy, along with alcohol.'

'*How old is she?*'

'She's 18. We've given her water. She's been sick but she's just stopped breathing.'

'*Is she breathing again?*'

(To Paul: 'Is she breathing?') '*No!*' 'She's not breathing.'

'*I've got the ambulance on its way to you now. Have you got her flat on her back on the floor?*'

'Yes, my husband's giving her mouth-to-mouth.'

'*Right, what's he doing? Can you tell me exactly what he's doing?*'

'Yes, he's a police officer, so he's trained in mouth-to-mouth, and I'm a nurse.'

'*Oh right, OK, so he knows what he's doing then. We're on our way to you now.*'

Although Leah had, in fact, not had any alcohol, I felt I had to cover that possibility. Paul was continuing to try to get Leah breathing again. I tried to help him. Every now and again some liquid was coming into Leah's mouth so I was helping Paul to drain it so he could continue resuscitating her.

Suddenly she vomited and Paul got some of it in his mouth. The shock of it prompted Paul to look up at me with such despairing eyes. 'I can't do this any more,' he said. Paul has a real aversion to sickness. He looked so distraught. I emptied Leah's mouth and took over.

In the meantime Sy, one of the lads who had come to the party, came upstairs to see what was going on. He was exceedingly calm.

He tried to talk to Leah. 'Come on, Leah,' he was saying to her as he looked for her pulse. He found it. Leah's heart never stopped beating, although her breathing had. I was still expecting Leah to cough and come round, but she didn't. I was still giving mouth-to-mouth resuscitation when the police arrived.

Downstairs, the lads had gone into 999 mode. Our house, as we have said, is in an isolated position, not an easy place for an ambulance driver to find. A couple of the lads had opened the gates ready for its arrival and a couple of the others had run down the road to look out for it. It seemed like forever until the ambulance arrived, but it was probably only about five minutes.

The ambulancemen came upstairs and took over, while I used the manual ventilator (the Ambubag). They had to strip Leah's top half to attach all the monitors that measured her heart-rate. Paul went downstairs to help bring up the cradle required to transfer Leah to the ambulance.

Downstairs, there were pockets of people. The girls were crying and the boys were subdued. Paul went downstairs once again and, in his words, went apeshit. 'Which one of you bastards gave Leah that tablet? I need to know. My daughter is dying upstairs!'

He was escorted firmly, but nicely, from the room by one of the police officers. 'Leave it with us, mate. We'll sort it all out, you go back upstairs with your daughter.'

Quite sensibly, Sarah had said nothing. If she had, I don't know what Paul would have done to her. By the time he got upstairs, Leah was strapped into the cradle, her breathing still being done for her. She was, although we did not know it, already dead.

PAUL: Leah was transferred to the ambulance. Jan got in with her. I was left behind. The walk back from the gate down our long driveway was one of the longest I have ever had. I had never felt so alone, except for the time I was beaten up at that wedding. My mind was all jumbled up, my world had disintegrated.

I telephoned Norman, the partner of Jan's oldest daughter Wendy, to tell them the news. At the time Wendy was on night duty in a psychiatric unit at Broomfield Hospital, Chelmsford – the very hospital where Leah was about to be taken. We needed someone to look after William who was by now very upset indeed. He was only 11 years old and had seen everything that had happened. A policewoman took him under her wing.

I was not allowed into the lounge, probably for the guests' protection. A police officer assured me that they would see William would be OK and they would wait until Norman arrived to pick him up and take him to the hospital. In the meantime, Norman had telephoned Wendy to let her know what had happened. The police told me they would lock up for me. Besides, they still had some unfinished business to take care of.

The guests were searched. Sarah produced two other pills – she and Leah had purchased four altogether. A couple of the lads were found with cannabis in their possession and were nicked. I was then put into a police car and rushed to Broomfield Hospital to be reunited with Leah and Jan.

JANET: In the ambulance Leah was on the bed behind the driver with his assistant still 'bagging' her to keep her breathing. I was sitting on the opposite side, strapped in, which seemed very unnatural: I felt I should be doing something to help. The ambulanceman remained quite calm, concentrating on what he had to do.

The journey to the hospital took about half an hour. We were met by a policeman. He put his arm around me as Leah was taken to the resuscitation room. I was taken to the sister's office. My legs were like jelly and I felt numb. I wanted to cry but I couldn't. I desperately wanted Paul to turn up. The policeman stayed with me. He was lovely.

A doctor came in after a while to see me. 'We've put your daughter on a ventilator. We're going to take her through now to do a brain scan. We think there is some cerebral swelling.'

That's when it hit me and I burst into tears. Leah was wheeled out of the resuscitation room connected to a ventilator. She was still 'unconscious'. I was still hoping against hope they would come along and tell me 'She's OK now, she's conscious. You can take her home in a few days'. But they didn't.

Medically, I had some idea of what was going on. Leah was still being scanned when Paul arrived. We waited together in the sister's office before going down to the Intensive Treatment Unit to see Leah. Before we went in we were warned how hard it is to see someone you love in this situation.

Leah was connected to the ventilator and had a catheter attached to her. I had seen this sort of thing before at first hand on several occasions. Paul hadn't. It was so hard for him. It was for me, too. It's so different when it's one of your own family lying there.

Poor Paul, he was still feeling guilty about not carrying on with resuscitation in our bedroom after Leah had vomited. As he said: 'My daughter's life was ebbing away in front of me and, because of some stupid quirk of mine, I just couldn't carry on.'

I was questioning myself, too. After all, here I was, a trained nurse. Surely I should have done more? Surely I should have known what to do? When someone goes into collapse I had been trained to go through the list – the airway, the breathing, the circulation, are they going into shock, are they doing this, are they doing that. I hadn't been able to think logically.

I said to the consultant, Dr John Durcan, 'What did I do wrong?'

He looked straight back at me and said: 'Mrs Betts, if I had been at the party myself, I would have done exactly the same. There was nothing else you could have done.'

Because he said it with such sincerity and conviction, he helped to put my mind at rest to some degree, although I shall wonder about it for the rest of my days.

3

Praying for a Miracle

JANET: **Sunday, November 12**. In the morning, Wendy, Norman, and Emily turned up at the hospital. Wendy had telephoned my mother in the early hours, who then gave Emily the news. Then they telephoned Cindy at Sheffield University, who said she would get the first train down to us. Two long-time friends of ours, Peggy and Hugh Rees, who live in Romford, took Paul home so he could feed the animals and dogs. This became a daily journey for Hugh throughout the time Leah was in the hospital.

I stayed with Leah. Paul had a shower and a change of clothing and picked up some money. He telephoned Chris to tell him what had happened. Chris was quite emotional. 'I've just got through all this with Dot,' he said. 'I can't take all this as well.' Poor Chris. He only came to the hospital once, stayed for a short while and then left. We could quite understand why. Not everyone can handle such a situation; everyone is different.

When Paul arrived home, all the party food was still out and all the furniture was still in the wrong rooms, but that was how it was left. This was no time to be doing housework. Paul returned to the hospital.

The medics had explained to us what was going on most of the time and answered most of our queries reasonably frankly, although obviously they were sensitive.

When I heard them talking at the end of Leah's bed, saying they would do this, or do that and discussing drugs and dosages, and such like, I think I knew in my heart of hearts what had happened, even though I wanted a miracle to happen and was still talking to Leah and playing tapes to her. The medics obviously were hoping to let us down gently by allowing us to come to our own conclusions about Leah's condition. We didn't want to leave Leah at all, not even to go to the toilet, just in case something happened while we were away.

During the afternoon, Leah had a visitor. It was Sarah. Her father had brought her along. The police liaison officer at the hospital, Peter Laurie, came to see us. He told us Sarah would like to see Leah and did we have any objection? How could we refuse? Leah and Sarah had been inseparable. By this time we were beginning to realise that nobody had forced Leah to swallow the tablet – it had been Leah's own choice.

Although Sarah had taken one of the same tablets as Leah, physically she seemed OK. Mentally though, it was another matter. She was like a zombie. She hadn't slept all night and was terrified at what we might say to her. But, more than anything else, she was worried about her friend. Her poor father was in a terrible state. He kept apologising to us, time and time again.

Throughout the time Leah was in the hospital, Sarah stayed at Leah's bedside all day long every day, and would have stayed all night as well if we had let her. She went through hell. As she sat there she was telling Leah all the news about their friends and talking about the holiday they spent together in Spain, anything she could think of. She put headphones on Leah and played Oasis tapes. At first we found it hard to feel sorry for her but, towards the end, it was impossible not to. We were losing our daughter; Sarah was losing her best friend.

We were allowed to stay with Leah all the time. We could talk to her, sing to her, play her tapes if we wanted to. The staff didn't mind what we did. We could have stood on our heads naked so long as it wasn't detrimental to Leah's care. The thought passed through my mind as to what kind of life we would have if Leah was to regain consciousness but be handicapped because of brain damage. We would have to look after her, but how would we cope? I felt sure that Leah would rather die than end like that. Such thoughts made me feel so guilty.

They were giving Leah large doses of diuretic to make her body excrete water and increase her urine output, and also Mannitol, which is often used in cases where the brain swells. Leah had general nursing care – apart from the blood samples which were taken to Guy's Hospital poisons unit to see if there were any toxins in her system other than Ecstasy.

We are fortunate to have such good friends. One of them, Andy Hamill, turned up. He was a student at Reading University. He had been travelling back to Reading from Essex when the news of a girl who had taken Ecstasy came over the radio. When he heard our names, he immediately turned his car around and drove straight to the hospital. He was wonderful and stayed with us for three weeks after Leah died, becoming our PR man, and handling all the hundreds of press calls coming into our home. We don't know what we would have done without him. Gone mad, most probably. Meanwhile, Peggy and Hugh had taken William back to their home in Romford to look after him for the next few days.

Two other friends, Alan and Jill Rose, played their part as well. They went to our home and tidied everything up for us, putting all the furniture back. Alan runs UK Transplant Limited, an organ-donation organisation. He takes teams all over the country and abroad, to remove organs and take them to patients who need them. The thought of coming to see Leah under similar circumstances was too much for him, so he didn't come into the hospital.

The police press liaison officer, Peter Laurie, came to see us in the waiting room at the ITU. Stephanie Martin, the PR lady at Broomfield Hospital, was with him. 'The press have got hold of all this. There's obviously great interest,' she said, 'our phones just haven't stopped ringing.'

Peter told us: 'I used to be a journalist, so I know how they can behave. In this case I don't think they will, but if you feel you can talk to them, this might be a good opportunity to do so. Let me arrange a well-organised press conference here, in the hospital. I will make sure they all behave themselves. If they don't I'll get them out. It's better than going home and finding them all at your front door.'

We agreed. It was at this moment Paul had an inspired idea. 'I don't know what we can say to them,' he said. 'A picture of Leah lying there, connected by a tube to a ventilator, could say more than I ever could.' He was so right. I asked Peter Laurie if this could be arranged. Dr Jo Davis remembered there was a Polaroid camera in the operating theatre. And so it was decided to take Leah's photograph. Jo went to fetch the camera and Paul took the now famous photograph that was eventually to appear in every newspaper and on television.

The time came to go into the area prepared for the press conference. We were amazed at how many people were there. It was unbelievable. We had only expected to see half a dozen or so reporters, but there were flash guns going off, television cameras, the lot.

To their credit, they all behaved impeccably and with courtesy. Perhaps some of them were parents themselves and were thinking, 'There, but for the grace of God, go I'. Some of them were obviously upset when they saw us. Peter told us if we got too emotional we could leave at any moment and we didn't have to answer any questions we didn't want to.

The press had taken over the whole quadrangle of the hospital. Their vans were outside with satellite dishes and there was a huge crowd of reporters. We were so nervous about facing them but they were marvellous. We wondered if they would bother us if we wanted to stretch our legs in the grounds or when we went to the canteen. They didn't. Even when they saw us, they just left us alone, prepared to wait for the next press conference. Not one of them invaded our privacy.

Later, when Paul and I popped outside for a breath of air in the hospital grounds, we passed an ambulance near the casualty department. There were two ambulance personnel in it, awaiting their next passenger. One of them looked across at all the pressmen in the quadrangle in the middle of the hospital and observed: 'Don't know what all the fuss is about. It's her own bloody fault, she shouldn't have taken it.'

At the time it upset me, but now I understand the truth of his remark. In fact, his comment has stayed with Paul and me and it has become the crux of our whole attempt to promote the entitlement of everyone to know the whole truth about these drugs. Leah made her own decision to take Ecstasy. No one held her down and shoved the pill down her throat. But I know, from conversations with her friends since, she knew only half the story – the half which the commercial world surrounding drug taking, the people earning the money from it in whatever form, wished her and thousands like her to know.

THAT IS WHAT ALL THE BLOODY FUSS IS ABOUT!

Monday, November 13: The only person I really felt able to express my fears to was my friend Peggy Rees. We decided to get out of the hospital for a while. We went outside to get some fresh air. I said to her, 'She's dead, isn't she, Peggy? She's not going to recover.'

Peggy and I don't pull our punches when we're together. 'I think you're right,' she replied. 'I don't think she'll recover.'

That helped because I could say it to her, whereas I just couldn't snatch Paul's ray of hope away from him. I didn't want mine taken away from me either – but deep down I knew. Later that day, one of the doctors, John Durcan, came to see us and intimated that the longer things went on as they were, the less hope there was.

We received so many messages and gifts at the hospital, annointed cloths, medallions with Mary and Christ on them, rosaries, whatever people thought would help. A man telephoned who practises ACCESS. This is a process used on people in comas to help guide them back to consciousness by talking to them and physically giving them information. For instance, taking the patient's hand and saying 'Can you feel the bed?' and placing their hand on the bed. Then you would say 'Thank you. Everything is all right, you are nice and comfortable in bed. You're warm, feel how warm you are', and then you would place their hand on their warm body.

The idea is to orientate the patient if they are trying to find their way back to consciousness. Paul tried this method. He was willing to try absolutely anything to bring Leah back, anything at all in the hope of a miracle. That night, Paul slept in a chair by Leah's bed. There was also a room down the corridor with two beds, and I spent some of the night in there.

Tuesday, November 14: We were told that there had been so much publicity about Leah's situation that the hospital had taken on an extra telephonist to handle all the calls. It was the same in the ITU. In the end, they would allow only family calls to come through. Wendy, Cindy, Emily and my mother were spending most of the days with us and other friends popped in and out. William also visited Leah, but only for short spells as it was too much of an ordeal for an 11-year-old to stay in all the time.

Dr Alasdair Short, a tall, rather abrupt Scotsman, came to us and said, 'There's been no change in Leah's condition. We have carried out several tests but nothing's happened. I don't think there's much hope for the future.' That's when Paul began asking me more questions. I think, by now, the penny had dropped.

Throughout all the time we had been with Leah in the hospital there had been something bearing heavily on my mind, something I hadn't felt able to share with Paul. Leah's mother Dot had chosen not to have Leah baptised. She felt baptism should be the individual's choice, a choice to be made when they are old enough to make a considered decision.

Although Paul and I are not exactly bible bashers, we are both Christians and I was so worried that Leah had not been baptised. I just didn't know how I should let Paul know how I felt. However, unknown to me, Paul was thinking along the same lines. Don Gordon, our local vicar, was also a friend and Paul decided to ask him to come to the hospital to say a prayer for Leah. Don readily agreed and came within a couple of hours.

Leah's bed was screened off to give us some privacy. As Don stood by the bed he asked us if there was anything special we wanted him to say. It was almost like telepathy as Paul said: 'Will you baptise her?'

Don looked taken aback. 'Yes, of course I will.'

Leah's named nurse Barbara was also a Christian who had recently lost her brother. She was still hurting from his death, so we invited her to join us. There were just the four of us there with Leah. Don baptised her and laid on hands.

We all had tears streaming down our faces, but when Don baptised Leah there was a peace within me and I felt she would be all right, even if she died. Don told us afterwards that, at the point when he put the cross on Leah's head it 'stood out' and he knew this was not going to be the end. 'Something would come of this, things would go further.' It was such a relief for us to know, that spiritually at least, Leah was going to be OK.

Wednesday, November 15: Paul contacted Alan Anthony, another of his friends. Alan practises faith healing. Now whether you believe in these things or not, when faced with a situation such as we were in, you will try anything. I have seen the way healing can bring peace to people before – a bond with your own particular beliefs.

The ITU staff gave us all the privacy we needed as Alan led me through quite a profound experience. I suppose some experts in psychology would say that my mental anguish at the time made me particularly susceptible, but I don't really care: I know what I experienced, whatever the reason, and it was beautiful – a reinforcement of my religious conviction that Leah was on the road to Heaven, to a peaceful place full of light and hope.

Alan and I were in a quiet place, in private, in Paul's presence, and we held hands. The scene I saw had a blue aura about it and it appeared that Leah was in a tunnel – not an oppressive, dark tunnel, but surrounded by light. She was in a white robe, floating first forwards, then back slightly, but always progressing towards the light. She looked so peaceful and happy, as though she really wanted to make it to the end of the tunnel. She kept reaching back to me and smiling.

I told Alan what I had seen. He said blues and greens were the colour of peace, and that I knew what I must do. I did know. Either she would be willed back, with God's help, or encouraged to complete her journey to Him. It was one of the most profound experiences of my life. No one can ever take it away, and please ... I don't want it psychoanalysed!

The doctors came back to see us: 'We've got to carry out more tests.' They suspected brain-stem death and another test would have to be done again later in the day. If there was no change after the second test, we were told it would be assumed there was brain-stem death, and there would be no way back for Leah. She was wheeled away for the first test. We had never prayed so much in all our lives. But it was in vain. By the end of the day we were given the news we had been dreading. Leah was brain-stem dead.

PAUL: It was the news that finally drove me to 'kick God into touch'. I was going through every possible emotion and was so angry that God could let this happen. There was my daughter. She was warm. She was beautiful and unmarked. She had a lovely colour to her and her chest was going up and down. How could He let this happen?

One of Leah's feet became uncovered and I just stroked it from top to bottom with my finger. Suddenly, her toes curled right up. I was overjoyed, 'Yes, we've cracked it, we're there!'. I thought – only to be told this was just a natural reflex. The body didn't need a brain to do that. I felt so deflated because I thought there was hope after all. I'd heard some coma patients do nothing for years, then one day wake up demanding their breakfast. Why couldn't my daughter do that?

Thursday, November 16: Because of the result of Leah's second brain-stem test, the decision whether or not to leave her on the respirator was taken away from us. When we saw Dr Short, Jan said to him: 'My God, I don't know if we can make this decision.' We were told, politely, it was not our decision to make, but that, before the machine was switched off, we could have all the time we needed to say our goodbyes to Leah.

If I were asked if I would have wanted the machine to be left on, I would have said yes. After all, as long as Leah was there, I had hope. I know it was a stupid hope – after all, her brain was dead. But Leah looked alive, perfect. It wasn't like she had been in an accident, there were no marks on her. Apart from the tube making her breathe, she looked so normal. If ever we had to trust a team of doctors, this was the time.

A few weeks earlier, Leah had decided to answer an appeal on BBC Essex, our local radio station, for people to carry donor cards. They were after 100 names to add to the register. Leah telephoned the station but was told that, at 17 years of age, she was not old enough to carry one. She was very disappointed. Now, so soon after that disappointment, her body was about to be taken into an operating room to be prepared for organ donation.

We had told the medics of Leah's wish to become a donor. The moment at which the machine was to be switched off had to be timed precisely, so that the various transplant teams were ready to remove the organs. The machine was scheduled to be switched off in the early hours of the morning. Leah was put into a room on her own before being taken into the operating room. That's when it really hit us. The family had gathered to say their goodbyes. The nurses were reluctant to allow William to be alone in the room with Leah but he insisted, almost pushing one of the nurses out of his way.

While William was in the room, we were aware of Dr Short becoming very angry with someone on the other end of a telephone line in the background. Apparently, the Home Office pathologist needed tissue samples and could they take them before the organs were being donated? Dr Short was shouting into the telephone: 'Do you really think I am going to put this family through all this for another 24 hours because you can't take your tissue samples?'

He was insistent that everyone had gone through enough, and that included the staff.

JANET: When William came out, the family went home. Paul was desperate that Leah should not be alone at the time she physically died, but he could not face going into the operating room. I didn't want to either but, because of my nursing experience of operating theatres, I decided to do this one last thing for Paul, and Leah.

When Vanessa, the transplant co-ordinator, came to see us I asked her if I could accompany Leah into the operating room. Although this was an unusual request, Vanessa agreed I could, but only after warning me about the sights and sounds I should expect when in the operating room. I explained I had worked in theatre before and was familiar with the kind of atmosphere I should expect to find in there. Vanessa offered to arrange to put up a screen so all I would see would be Leah's head.

We had to wait for the porters to take Leah from the room into the operating theatre. It seemed to take forever. There was a quite different atmosphere in the room. The machine Leah was now connected to was much noisier. It was very awkward trying to say goodbye to Leah because of the noise coming from the large bellows and because of all the tubes attached to her. Wendy, Cindy and Emily were all crying. I remember telling Leah I loved her, not to worry, she'd be all right. I know that sounds a daft thing to say, but that's the way it came out. I stroked her hair. Paul kissed her and said his goodbyes, and I gowned up. Leah was wheeled away.

During a transplant, the organs that need oxygenating have to be removed first. Leah's kidneys and liver were therefore removed first of all. Then, after what seemed like ages, they at last allowed me into the operating room. The cardiac monitor was on one side of Leah, with the anaesthetist, and I was on the other. The aorta, the large artery of the heart, was about to be clamped. When this was done, Leah's heart would stop, and the line on the monitor would go flat.

When I went in, I stroked Leah's cheek. She was already very pale. I bent and kissed her damp forehead and whispered 'Night-

night Leapy.' [Leapy was her nickname, as in Leapy Lee.] 'You'll be all right, I promise.' I could not see her body because of the screens.

At 6.03 am, when her aorta was clamped, Leah suddenly felt cold and clammy, like a heart-attack victim, and the monitor went flat. At the same time, blood poured down a tube into a bucket by my feet. It was Leah's life blood draining away right in front of me and it haunts me to this day.

Very distressed, I left, held up by Vanessa, to be reunited with Paul. He claimed he had experienced something like an electric shock at the precise time Leah's heart had stopped. I thought 'Oh God, is she really dead?' If I had said to the doctors, 'You are not going to do this,' they would have had to stop. But I didn't.

When the transplant teams had finished their work, Paul and I were allowed to go in to see Leah. She was lying there, covered with a sheet up to her shoulders. She was so pale, so colourless. I stood there thinking 'Oh God, what have I done?' It's a feeling I am sure will never ever go away.

The only consolation we had from Leah's death was that her organs would be helping six or seven people start a new life, and possibly someone would be helped to see again. Leah's liver, both kidneys, her spleen, heart and lungs, both corneas and her windpipe were donated.

One thing has to be emphasised, though. At the time it is dreadful, but Leah was treated with respect at all times and, after all, when the funeral is over and done with, what is left? It was Leah's wish to donate her organs if anything happened to her. In retrospect, although it was the hardest decision we ever had to make, it was also one of the best.

Leah will never have her own children, yet we know that five people live on, two people can see and a baby's life has been saved because of her. She lives on with them and their families. When the reality of what is left of Leah hits home, you realise what a waste it would have been not to have carried out her wish.

To those recipients I say: 'Don't have any negative feelings, only very positive ones. Whoever you are, live long and happy.' To any other relative who should find themselves in a similar position to us, when the initial grief is over, I would say: 'You won't ever regret your decision.'

Four hours later, at 10 am, we faced the press again. It was our decision to do so. By now we had built up a rapport with the pressmen. They had been rooting for Leah, even though they were there to do a job. In fact, they had become a support to us. We needed to tell them we had carried out Leah's wishes. We needed to tell the whole country we had because we had received letters from far and wide from people rooting for her. I suppose we felt we could show people that, as well as carrying out Leah's wishes, we had got through it. Perhaps that would encourage other people to do the same thing.

Leah was taken to the Chapel of Rest in the hospital grounds. Dr Jo Davis led us around the back way to avoid the pressmen. She had, in fact, officially identified Leah to save us from going through more anguish. Our other daughters were with us, and so was William. It was a neat enough place. Leah was in a coffin, in a nightie. She looked so beautiful, but it was so cold. If it had been a respectful thing to do, and if it had crossed my mind at the time, I would have photographed her there.

It is when the pro-drug-taking lobby blithely say 'But there's not been that many deaths, has there?' that I get so mad. I could shove that picture in their faces and say, 'This, *this*, is real life, mate. Don't call my daughter a statistic. She *does* matter. Not just to us – she SHOULD matter to you as well because, however much you think your name is not on the next pill, it's like the big golden finger: it could be you.'

I remember being asked by Judy Finnegan on ITV's 'This Morning' programme the following day, what it was I would always remember. One of those things was that scene. Leah was such a pale, cream colour, and so cold. We all stood there, grieving, but it was somehow unreal, detached. I can remember the tears in Judy's eyes as I answered, and I thought 'She knows what I mean, she's seen it at some time.'

4

Life Without Leah

JANET: A few hours after Leah's machine was switched off, we arrived home. It was bedlam. The first person I can remember seeing when I walked into our lounge was Dr Southey, our local general practitioner. Although he was not a family friend as such, he had been a wonderful support to Paul after he was attacked and had come to visit us on the Christmas morning, even though he wasn't on duty, when Paul's mother died. I was so pleased to see him. His support was there for us. I just went up and cuddled him. It was really nice he took the bother to come.

Jason Nicholls, a television producer from Granada TV, turned up and so did Sue Harris, a BBC producer. The telephone was ringing non-stop, keeping our friend Andy Hamill busy. Sue asked us if we would be prepared to appear on a television programme *that night* in a Norwich studio. We had hardly slept for hours but, she said, 'There's no need to worry, we'll drive you there and back. You can sleep throughout the journey.' We agreed to go along.

The car picked us up. It was a terrible journey, roadworks and raining all the way. On the programme we appeared on a panel with the mother of a lad who had died after using the drug speed, a police officer from Norfolk, and a pro-cannabis lobbyist. We were interviewed by Kim Riley, the presenter. He was brilliant, really nice. We had never been in a television studio before but it was to be the first of many, many more such occasions.

The following morning, we were at the other end of the country, at the Granada Television studios in Liverpool, appearing on the *This Morning* programme. The whole family came with us and, that evening, we were on television yet again, on Central Television's *Live*, a type of 'Bear Pit' programme, where we faced some drug pushers.

That day was an experience in itself and the seeds of an idea were beginning to come to us. We were in a position to do something positive about the menace of drugs in our society. We had a powerful message and we could use the media exposure given us to good effect. We had done some radio interviews at the hospital and now we realised just how big this issue was becoming. If so many newspapers and radio and television stations wanted to speak to us, we were in a good position to warn other youngsters against making the same choice as Leah.

We had not realised until now just how much media coverage Leah's plight had aroused while we were at the hospital. In the ITU we were cut off from the world. When we saw all the television vans with satellite dishes on top of them parked at the hospital, we had no idea of the scale of attention we were attracting, nor did we have any idea just how many people would be seeing us on their television screens in their homes.

We knew other kids had died after taking Ecstasy. We couldn't understand why Leah's case had attracted so much attention. Why had she been chosen? When Daniel Ashton from Blackpool and Debbie Warburton from Manchester died, there was some local coverage but nothing on this scale. We can only put it down to our willingness to talk to the media.

To some people, the thought of going from one place to another immediately after the death of a loved one, would be intolerable, but for us, it helped. We had experienced what it is like after other family bereavements, when the deceased was hardly mentioned in case of upsetting a close relative. We needed to talk about Leah in order to help us come to terms with her death.

The people in our village were very kind. They even held a

memorial service for Leah before the funeral. Don gave a strong sermon at the service, along the lines of justice will be done – if not in this world, then in the next. People will eventually know what is going on with this drug culture. We must not let the evil, callous dealers win. The power of Don's sermon helped to restore Paul's faith in God.

One of my friends, Sheila Lloyd, had recently lost her husband Trevor. Like me, Sheila is a straight talker and she could empathise with us. After Trevor's death, she said, it was upsetting if people were reluctant to mention Trevor's name to her when all she really wanted to do was to talk about him. She promised she would not do that to us.

As for our own family, Wendy had Norman's support. They could go away to cry or talk it out between themselves before coming back to talk it out again with us. Cindy, however, isn't one to show a lot of emotion, but I could tell she was really feeling it. Her way of dealing with Leah's death was to try not to talk about it more than she could help.

I think Emily felt it worst of all. She immediately came to stay with us from East London University. She remained for quite a while and felt very close to William. But every time she packed her bags to return to university, when she got to the bottom of the stairs she would say, 'It's no use, Mum, I can't face it. I can't go back.' She was like that for quite a while, which is not like her at all.

We received hundreds of letters after Leah died, the vast majority of which were very supportive, although we did receive a few 'weird' or cruel ones. It was quite an emotional experience to read them. Every day piles and piles of them arrived. We would split them into two heaps; Paul would read one heap and I would read the other. Then, when we had finished, we would swap over. Several MPs wrote to us, as did a couple of mediums and some television personalities who had had tragedies in their own lives.

When Leah had been in hospital, members of the pop group Take That telephoned. They wanted us to know they were thinking of us and was there anything they could do? I thought it was so kind of them. It was the lads themselves, not just a public relations man. Between them all, they had given us a tremendous feeling of support.

Leah had been taken from the hospital to a chapel of rest in Southminster. Paul, William and I went there to visit her after the post mortem. The girls couldn't face going. Several of Leah's friends had been before us. Inside Leah's coffin were several little things such as little toys and so on. William had painted her a picture and we put in a photograph of us all together, taken when William was dedicated at the church with Leah holding his hand.

Leah was wearing the clothes she had worn at the party – even the shoes – and her hair was brushed down as it was normally, not tied up as it had been in the hospital. They had put some make-up on her face and she looked quite nice. After seeing her as she had been at the hospital, this put Paul's mind at rest quite a lot. She looked 'normal' again, except now she was stone cold.

The funeral service was held on December 1 at our village church in Latchingdon, before burial at St Mary's Church in Great Burstead. Our church was packed for the service, everyone and their brother was there, plus a small army of cameramen and television crews. Don gave a marvellous service. William read a poem he had written for Leah, and Wendy and Leah's aunt, Kathleen Holmes, said a few words as well. Leah was brought into the church to the tune of 'Wonderwall' by Oasis. Many found Paul's metaphorical farewell to Leah particularly touching:

Quite a long time ago, a pretty little ship was created. Its owner looked down upon it with love and affection and was very proud as it was part of his blood, sweat and tears. It was perfect in every way. During the following years, he fitted the little ship out with radar, compass, lights, echo-sounder, radio and log. He thought he had prepared the little ship for anything the sea could throw at it, and it could communicate as and when needed. He trusted it with all his heart and believed that, wherever it went, it would return safely.

One day, the little ship was to enter unchartered waters, unbeknown to its captain. The evening started calmly with a gentle glow in the sky, and the little ship was decked out in all its splendour with a soft wind filling the sails, but it was not long before the little ship was in a full blown storm. It was tossed from wave to wave.

You could hear it cry out in pain as the sea bashed against its sides and made its ribs groan under the strain. Its captain fought to maintain control, but the sea had taken charge of the little ship and the captain was powerless to do anything. He could only sit in the cockpit and watch as his beautiful little ship tried to weather the storm.

All of a sudden, a gigantic wave lifted the little ship into the air and tossed it onto jagged rocks. The little ship's timbers split and it shuddered under the strain of the sea's constant hammering. Then, just as quickly as it had begun, the storm passed and all was quiet.

The captain looked at his pretty little ship, now motionless and silent upon the rocks. He could see the damage the sea had done and tried to patch the holes so the little ship would be alive and float again, but it was all in vain. His little ship was lost and would never sail the sea.

The captain's heart was heavy. It appeared all his preparation had been in vain. 'Why, oh why?' he thought, but no answer came. He now felt so alone and helpless looking at his lifeless little ship. As he lifted his head in sorrow, he could see other little boats coming towards him from an island. The people took his hand and gave him support and comfort.

They took him and carefully carried his little ship to the island where they placed it in a sandy harbour where the sea could do no more damage.

The captain looked at his little ship with love, affection and sadness and was preparing to say his fond farewell, when, something made him look along the coastline. There, he noticed other little ships that had been left high and dry, still greatly loved by their captains as they had been protected from the elements. They too were in need of repair but were not in such a bad state as his little ship.

One of the ships needed a new keel, mast and sails. These were the heart and lungs of the ship, another needed a compass, another lights, another radar to see. He realised his little ship could provide all the essential parts to repair these other boats.

The captain told the islanders his thoughts. They were overjoyed. They came to his little ship and, with great love, affection and compassion, removed the vital parts needed for the other boats. It was not long before six boats from along the coastline were back at sea, enjoying a new lease of life, being free again. These boats also brought a breath of fresh air and hope to their owners, who had almost given up hope of ever going back to sea again.

The captain went back to the sandy harbour and looked down upon his once pretty little ship. All that remained was the bare hull, its very being had been removed. He then turned and looked out to sea and saw the repaired boats sailing and, although his heart was sad at the loss of his cherished little ship, he felt pride for her as he saw her living on in the other boats, and therefore she would be remembered, not only by him but by many other families which she had helped.

He then turned back to his little ship and whispered the words from the title of a famous song: 'I WILL ALWAYS LOVE YOU.'

He knew now his pretty little ship was truly at peace and, with one last glance, he turned and walked away.

The hymns 'All Things Bright and Beautiful', 'In Heavenly Love Abiding', 'Jerusalem', 'Fight the Good Fight' and Psalm 23 were sung; then, at the end of the service, the theme tune from *The Bodyguard* 'I Will Always Love You' was played. We thought it appropriate, because of the words and especially as it had been the film we had been watching at the party. I am told there was hardly a dry eye in the church, pressmen included. It was such an emotional moment.

Leah was buried alongside her mother. Even now, the thing I hate most of all, when we visit her grave, is coming away and leaving her there. If I could have picked her up and taken her home in my arms, I would have done so. She would have been all right then, wouldn't she? We would put her to bed to recover, and she would wake up in the morning as normal, and so would we. Except she wouldn't and we wouldn't. It tears at you when you have to go, but you know you must.

At the cemetery, the only people allowed to film were the cameramen from Granada Television, the result of an arrangement between us following our appearance on the *This Morning* programme the day after Leah died. After that programme, Granada received a record number of telephone calls.

By coincidence, some British Telecom executives were at the studio that morning, British Telecom was sponsoring the programme concerned. As they had been making their way home afterwards on the train, four of the executives sat there and said, 'We really must do something about this.' They got together with some producers from Granada and came up with a plan. They got back to us later to ask how we felt about producing an educational video. We thought it was a good idea, not envisaging how it would turn out.

We thought we would have to stand holding bottles of pills saying things like 'This is what they look like', but it was not like that at all. The British Telecom executives had approached a producer called Sue Durkan and told her what they had in mind.

It was decided to call the video *Sorted*, which is an expression used in nightclubs by drug pushers. 'Are you sorted? Have you got your gear?' means 'Have you got your drugs?' I had told Sue that no actress in the world could ever re-enact how Leah died, no matter how good she was. Sue had decided though, to reproduce the party as if seen through Leah's eyes. We agreed and they arranged to come to the house. Before they arrived, they had filmed at the hospital, at Leah's college and the police headquarters. Then they took over our home.

Wendy and Emily were there but Cindy couldn't come because she was taking her exams in Sheffield. Sarah came and so did some of Leah's other friends. They were all interviewed. At one o'clock in the morning, they were still at it and I was busy making everyone bacon sandwiches. Part of the video was to feature the funeral. The idea was to complete the filming, edit the video and distribute a copy to every secondary school in the United Kingdom before the Christmas holidays – a fair feat indeed! Granada supplied the production facilities and British Telecom the finance.

The end result was nothing like what we had expected but it was brilliant nevertheless. It was intended primarily to be a teaching tool and was sent out with a letter from television personalities Richard Madeley and Judy Finnegan and from us, together with an evaluation form. There were between 50,000 and 60,000 replies of the form which, we were later told, produced some very valuable research material.

The effect of *Sorted* is always quite stunning. There is always a silence at the end of the showing. It helps to make youngsters realise that by taking drugs, it is not just their own lives that are affected but the lives of their families and friends, too.

Leah's death had sparked off a series of calls to the police. Hundreds telephoned with information about the drug culture in the area and the police had to set up a special incident room. All this information had to be collated. It transpired that Leah's supplier may, quite unwittingly, have had connections with dealers at the very top of the drug market. A few weeks later, three alleged dealers were shot dead in our area – but that is a part of the story to feature later in this book.

In December we were contacted by Paul Delaney, the managing director of Leach, Knight and Delaney, a large advertising company. He had been speaking to his colleagues and had designed a poster which he thought might help our cause. He had various hoarding sites on offer free of charge. Were we interested? Well, of course we were. Mr Delaney asked if he could come to see us and bring the poster. Basically, it was a black poster the size of a hoarding board. In the middle of the left two thirds of the poster was the word 'Sorted ...' and the right hand third had a smiling picture of Leah with the caption underneath reading 'One tablet took Leah Betts'. Initially, Paul Delaney had told us, he had 800 sites available. We were very grateful, especially when we heard we had use of the sites for a month, free of charge, which normally would have cost a million pounds to occupy!

Paul's motive? He was a dad and he didn't ever want to go through what we had gone through. He just wanted to do his bit to help. Later, moreover, a further 700 sites were made available – a total of 1,500 boards giving two million pounds worth of advertising space, other hoarding companies having come on board. And, instead of a month, the posters remained on display for considerably longer.

The first poster we saw was at Maldon (Essex), near the Tesco supermarket, almost overlooking where our yacht was moored. We were not expecting to see it and, initially, it upset us to see Leah displayed so publicly. After a while, though, we were comforted to think our daughter's plight might be helping to make other kids aware of the dangers of drugs. Because we travel so much, the following few months saw us all over the country and, just about everywhere we went, there was our beloved Leah looking down on us from a billboard.

The poster had a significant effect on my mother. Being a generation further down the line, she was still feeling stigmatised by the drug induced death of Leah. However, one Sunday, while travelling on an underground train at Becontree, near London, she saw the poster. I think it brought home reality to her. 'Why on earth am I feeling this way?' she thought. 'There was my poor granddaughter and now someone is trying to do something about it.' I think it just came to her when she saw the poster and, from then on, she was quite proud of what we were trying to do.

Emily, I know, found looking at the poster very difficult. William was also upset at first but, because the poster near Tesco was situated near a roundabout we frequently use, he began to get used to seeing Leah there and in fact, often waved and said 'Hello, Leah' as we drove by. In the end, I think he was quite disappointed one day when we drove past, to see Leah had been replaced by an advertisement for cigarettes.

After Leah died I began, just occasionally, to scribble my thoughts down in my diary. Looking back at those entries, it is plain to see the strain we were under at the time. Over the Christmas/New Year period I made several entries. For instance:

Monday, December 25, 1995. Dear Diary, It is one o'clock in the morning. Have we done the right thing going public or is all we have achieved to have the whole teenage population laughing at us? Does it matter? We had to try! Was the donation right? Was she able to recover without us realising? Can this message be carried on? I worry for the whole young population. Yet another serious incident would reinforce everything. Is it right to advise on safe usage? It's curious how you can wax lyrical when you're distressed.

We would rather have buried our heads than go through the motions of Christmas, but we had to for William's sake. He kept asking us again and again when we were going to put the tree up. I kept putting it off because it was always William, helped by Cindy and Leah, who used to decorate the tree. In the end, he went upstairs to get the tree and put it up on his own. I hadn't the heart to go out Christmas shopping really, but it had to be done.

Christmas Day itself wasn't too bad. William opened his presents and we went to Leah's grave before going over to Wendy and Norman's for our Christmas dinner. It was quite nice, just the family. Cindy had come down from university and my mum was there too. At least with everyone present being family, we could cry whenever we wanted to, knowing everyone else would understand.

Tuesday, December 26, 1995. Dear Diary, It's your worst nightmare to lose a child. A feeling of emptiness comes over you. Paul found an injured bird and cried. A little wren. It was so tiny and helpless. It recovered and flew away. So happy.

The arrival of one unexpected visitor in the middle of the night proved most unnerving. We live in the middle of nowhere and to have someone banging on the door at such a time was very frightening. Although we had built up quite a good relationship with the media, one national daily newspaper had repeatedly asked us about who had received Leah's organs. We did not know and told them so each time they contacted us. What happened that night prompted this entry in my diary.

Thursday, December 28, 1995. Dear Diary, At one o'clock this morning a courier telephoned us from the village claiming he was lost. Then he turned up in the fog. He had a letter from the paper asking about organ donation. THEY DON'T GIVE UP! Very frightening, it could have been anybody at that time of night. Some of the press want a scoop. Offering money for names of the recipients, despicable! Leah was shown on Memories of '95 *on Anglia Television. Now, it seems, she is just a memory.*

On New Year's Eve we had a telephone call from some people who had a drug-related problem within the family. Basically, they didn't know what to do. The family came over to see us. We had planned to go to the football clubhouse in the village to see in the New Year.

We didn't feel like doing much at all really, but this was, at least, local. We invited the visiting family to come with us to the club. They were nice people and we had quite a pleasant evening, although we felt a bit awkward being among some people we did not know too well.

Everything was going quite well. There was a disc jockey playing the music that evening and, on the stroke of midnight, he put on Whitney Houston's 'I Will Always Love You'. Paul and I, and my friend Sheila Lloyd who had come along with us, just dissolved into tears. Every time we hear that tune it really tears at our hearts.

Monday, January 1, 1996. Dear Diary, Research has shown just how many of our up and coming students are existing on Ecstasy. If it is true, 50 per cent of those youngsters are on it. What of the future? People think you are over it if you can go on camera. Not so. TV is unreal. It is a world we would never normally have known. We must rise above our grief to do programmes for Leah's sake.

Tuesday, January 2, 1996. Dear Diary, We went to see Don. Paul felt so unworthy in church on Sunday he nearly walked out, so needed to talk. Don had good ideas about a parent's line, a column, advertising and fund-raising, etc.

Wednesday, January 3, 1996. Dear Diary, The day started at 8am when we were awoken by the telephone. It was a pressman telling us about

Helen Cousins, a 19-year-old who took one tablet on New Year's Eve and is now in a coma. Her mum and dad, Janet and Trevor, are still not known to us. The press and radio wanted our advice to them. We sent our love and support. We rang the hospital and left our telephone number. Janet Cousins rang us. It was wonderful. Helen is recovering. They did go on television but had a bad experience with the press and they're not too keen to do it again. A great shame, but they may do so in time. Got near to giving up this afternoon, wondering if we have any right to advise against drug taking with a coffee in one hand and a New Year's drink in the other! Fed up with hearing about 50 deaths a year. It's still 50 too many. Have we failed? We will fail some, but not all. Got a call from a mum in Nottingham saying her daughter and boyfriend told her that Leah's campaign had stopped between eight and 12 of them from going to a party and taking drugs.

Friday, January 5, 1996. Dear Diary, Helen is back in intensive care. I learned this after coming back from ordering her flowers. When I told Paul he said it had already been reported in the press that I wanted the ward number to send flowers. Good job I did! How the hell did they get hold of that? The newspaper has been pestering again about organ donation and meeting recipients. I remember how Paul's mum chose his name. She opened her bible at random and saw the words ' ... and Paul shall be a leader of men'. He certainly is. I took down the Christmas decorations, talking to Leah. I cried. I remember how Leah and Cindy used to do them with William putting his oar in.

Sunday, January 7, 1996. Dear Diary, Spoke to Helen's mum Janet. Helen is now in a high dependency unit under an ENT surgeon. She still has a tracheotomy. Filmed on Ljubljana (our yacht) for World in Action. Very reflective. Then we were filmed at home with newspapers of Helen.

Monday, January 8, 1996. Dear Diary, Went on Robbie Vincent programme. A very useful exercise, our first ever phone-in. It's encouraging to hear people are behind us. It is true that other things like alcohol and asthma kill more people, but that doesn't mean you give up, and also means that drugs must be a current worry to the general public.

The police had been investigating the source of the tablets Leah and Sarah had purchased and had charged two young men in connection with their investigations.

Wednesday, January 10, 1996. Dear Diary, Boys are on bail to appear for trial at Crown Court with judge and jury.

Monday, January 29, 1996. Dear Diary, I had a flash of inspiration on the loo as to why we went public. We would have to live with the stigma of our daughter dying of drugs anyway, and we're not ones to stick our heads in the sand. That's why we decided to go public, to get the discussion going.

On January 31, the inquest into Leah's death was held at the Shire Hall in Chelmsford. We went with Don and his wife Barbara. Central Television came along too. They were filming us all day in order to produce a documentary. Don parked some way from the Shire Hall so we had to walk from the shopping centre. All of a sudden, one of the pressmen spotted us and then several of them came rushing across the road with their cameras. By now, we had got to know quite a few of them.

We went into the hall with a feeling of dread. What would they tell us about Leah? The coroner came up to us and took us to one side. He said something along the lines of 'Take your time, we can read out your statements to save you from standing up there in front of everyone.'

There was a very sombre atmosphere in the coroner's court. We sat right at the front. We were asked a few questions. I had to describe Leah's eyes after she had taken the tablet.

It was upsetting also, to hear what she had taken before – Leah had experimented with speed and had tried cannabis. I sat there thinking we must not let this tarnish Leah. I was still proud of her. She was just an ordinary kid who had tried what lots of other kids had done. She was not a drug addict. All the same, I was very wobbly.

The Home Office pathologist was there, as was Dr John Henry

from Guy's Hospital, who was in charge of the Poisons Unit. They both gave their medical opinions. The pathologist said 'Leah died from Ecstasy poisoning. Anything else was a complication caused by Ecstasy.' If she had not taken the Ecstasy she would have come to no harm. I've heard some people since say Leah's liver packed up on her. That's rubbish. If it had, I pity the poor woman in Spain who received it! So there it was: Ecstasy poisoning – end of story.

The press had asked if we would speak to them when we came out. We agreed and were surprised to find they had organised themselves in a large semi-circle outside, ready to meet us. They threw loads of questions at us and we answered them all.

Our whole world had been turned upside down when Leah died. Paul had started up a fishing chartering business earlier in the year, after leaving the police force. One day we had been to West Mersea, where we had watched some fishing boats coming in and out of the harbour. I suggested to Paul he combined his hobby with a business venture – fishing trips, perhaps. Fishing trips at the time were quite expensive. I thought that if he could keep the price down, we might be able to make a go of it. It worked and things had been going quite nicely.

Then, in the summer holiday, we saw a boat in Suffolk taking people on river trips. I realised nobody was running any such business from Maldon on the River Blackwater, near where we live, although there used to be river trips there years before. We decided to pursue the idea. We were sure the local council would find some reason to say no, but the opposite was the case, they helped us all the way.

We rigged out Paul's fishing boat to make it suitable. However, the fishing trips became so popular we realised it was not big enough and we needed more cover, so later we bought a bigger boat in need of renovation.

Our plans to renovate the boat were thrown into chaos after Leah died. There were just not enough hours in the day to work on the boat and to fit in all the media work and to operate Action for Drugs Awareness, which we have since set up to keep our message alive.

Friday, February 2, 1996. Dear Diary, Princess Diana and Mohamed Al Fayed [owner of Harrods store in London] want to see the video. Paul backed up his Jaguar and ripped off its door. We are bickering, and I hate it. I wish we could have a month on a desert island!

Sunday, March 10, 1996. Dear Diary, Went to church. Felt awful. A dreadful, black depression, even though the sermon was great – as usual. 'Our strength in times of trouble.' Boy, do we need that now!

5

Brotherly Love

JANET: I hope William has learnt a lifetime's lesson as far as drugs are concerned. He has yet to go through his teenage years and all the problems of peer pressure that they bring. I worry about him, as many of the current adolescent trends, which could so easily escalate, are very dangerous. I pray that as time goes on, and his memory of this experience fades to some degree, he will not lose the ability to think back on his sister's tragically stupid decision.

He has had to go through a lot since Leah's death. He has been bullied at school – and done some bullying himself – but fortunately has had his teachers' understanding. In many ways, part of his character grew up in a hurry. He has travelled with us, heard us speak on drugs, even taken part himself. He has met many people and been to many places he would not have experienced had it not been for Leah.

William has never reached the full potential of his capabilities academically, but has always been very grown-up in his speech. If the tragedy has done anything for him, it has widened his horizons in a way that would not have happened otherwise, and made him realise he is as good as the next person. He has now seen that, underneath, most people are very much alike: whatever their gifts, their jobs, their prejudices, be they politicians, televisions stars or whatever, they are all members of the human family. Life is really what you make it.

William wants to be a cameraman, an ambition he had before Leah died, and he now has a far greater knowledge of what he wants to achieve. Many of the camermen we have become involved with have been very good to him, particularly 'Beeny', the BBC *Matter of Fact* cameraman, who let him loose on a digital camcorder – William's idea of heaven.

Perhaps most important, he has seen the members of the media as human beings, not just the side which people usually perceive. Many of them have kids his age, or are not far past his age themselves, and really empathised with him. There's no fooling kids, they know when a person is genuine. They can see through a media-hardened shell.

This is something he needs to hang on to to avoid becoming so callous or cynical that he loses empathy with the subject of his camerawork, because if that happened his feeling for the humanity of his stories, and his respect for his subject, would be lost.

Leah's death, the funeral and the inquest were an extremely traumatic period for Paul and me and, of course, for Cindy, Wendy and Emily. But we were all at an age when we could express our grief and share it with each other. We had the maturity to cope, to some extent at least, with our emotions. It is hard to imagine how those events could affect an 11-year-old boy. How could he come to terms with what he had witnessed?

We could provide an account of how William has coped with the sight of his sister being taken ill and what it was like for him to see her in hospital connected to a life support machine. William had been alone with Leah just before she was transferred to the operating theatre to be prepared for the transplant teams. He had seen her in the chapel of rest and had attended her funeral. We could describe all this – but we could hardly do justice to his feelings. Better, then, to let him tell it in his own words.

WILLIAM: Leah always had a big smile on her face and was a very comforting sister. She would always look after me if I was upset or unwell. She never shouted at me or got angry with me. I didn't know anything about drugs, except they were bad for you.

When I was in the primary school, I was about to go home. I was the last one out. A man was standing outside the school with black, curly hair and a jacket with a figure skiing on the back of it. He didn't seem to know what he was saying. I tried to walk past him but he asked me if I wanted to have a good time and commented that 'it must be boring in that school'.

He offered me a see-through packet with white powder in it. I got back behind the school fence quickly and waited for about five minutes, then I hurried home to tell my Dad. Dad called the police and they interviewed me.

Until Leah became ill I didn't know anything about Ecstasy, I just knew them as drugs, I didn't know they all had different names.

At Leah's party, Mum and Dad were in the kitchen, watching television. I popped in and out during the evening for something to eat. Leah kept taking her food back into the lounge, but she just wouldn't keep still. I had never seen her act that way.

Later, I heard a loud noise upstairs. When I went up, Leah was hanging over the washbasin being sick. One of her friends told me to get my parents. Ten minutes later, when I went back up, Leah had really changed. She was screaming her head off, 'Mummy, Mummy, help me!!' Mum told me to go and get a bowl. When I came back, Leah was even worse. I just stood there, staring. I didn't know what to say or what to do.

I had seen Leah take a tablet earlier in the evening, but I thought it was just a paracetamol. I came downstairs yet again. Everyone was asking 'How is she?' Dad came rushing downstairs with tears pouring from his eyes. Everyone was crying, and then the police arrived. When we heard the police sirens coming, one of the guests tried to give something to me: 'Here you are, just get rid of it.' I didn't know what he was talking about. I told a policeman what was said and they began to search and found something hidden behind the bushes in the garden. 'That's what we were looking for,' one of them said.

Then the ambulancemen arrived and went upstairs. When they brought Leah down, she was lying on a stretcher, with a blanket over her but her leg was dangling down. She didn't pick it back up. I thought, why doesn't she? I was with one of Leah's friends at the time. He told me to turn my back and not to look, so I did as I was told.

I didn't know what to think and I couldn't understand why Dad had asked Norman to come and fetch me. Obviously Leah had taken something really bad to make her that sick, but I hadn't a clue she had taken a drug. That just wasn't like Leah.

I had a funny feeling in my stomach, like when you've done something wrong and Dad has just found out. I felt very, very sorry for Leah having to go in the ambulance on her party night. It would have been bad any day, but especially on her party night when she was having such a good time.

The next morning, Wendy and Norman took me to the hospital. I had to put a sort of apron on before I went in to see Leah. When I went in, there was a noise from a machine making her breathe. That immediately made me cry. I was wondering why she couldn't breathe on her own. Mum and Dad were crying, too.

Dad explained to me what Leah had done but I couldn't believe it. Peggy and Hugh took me back to their house to stay with them. We put the television on. Leah was on every channel on the news. I didn't want to think it was Leah. I didn't want to believe it. Now I knew it was very serious. Over the next few days I kept thinking 'I hope she's going to make it', but I didn't really think she would. I tried to get it out of my head, but I couldn't.

Then, one day when we were at the hospital, a nurse and a doctor came into the room and asked Peggy to take me out into the corridor. I thought that was strange as I was one of the family. Peggy explained to me that Leah had probably died. When I went back, Dad was all jumbled up with his words. He didn't know what to say, so in the end, I just said 'I know'.

Leah was moved into another room. I wanted to be alone with her but the machine she was on now was very noisy. Dad kissed her and went out. It was difficult to hold Leah's hand because she had a thing over her thumb to take her pulse. That was the last time I saw Leah until we went to the chapel of rest. I don't think Leah suffered in the hospital. I think she died in Dad's arms at home.

I went to Leah's funeral. I had written her a poem. It was about a rose, Leah's favourite flower.

There was once a flower which dropped a seed and out of that came
*   a beautiful rose which stood out from all the other flowers.*
The lovely rose grew too close to a weed, which started to wrap
*   around it and, as it struggled to get free, the weed became too tight*
*   and the rose died.*
But in so doing, the rose dropped six seeds and, out of the six seeds
*   grew six other lovely roses.*
The father and the mother of the beautiful rose looked at their loved
*   one, then looked at the six other roses and said, Thank you.*

The seeds in my poem were the organs Leah donated. As I read the poem at Leah's funeral, Dad was cuddling me. I didn't like the funeral because, when we got there, there were loads of cameras everywhere. There were no cameras allowed in the church, though, just the Granada Television cameraman making the *Sorted* video. There were a lot of people outside, listening to the service and there was a really huge crane with a camera on top, looking down at us. When we got to Leah's grave, we threw in some roses we had bought. Then we said goodbye and came away.

When I went back to school after the funeral my friends were very good to me, but some of the bullies tried to wind me up, saying nasty things about Leah. I've got a problem. I can't just walk away. I have to argue with them. One day, one of them wound me up so much I hit him. He told the teacher. She let me off but told me I had to learn not to do it again.

I do miss Mum and Dad when they go away with their Drugs Awareness campaign but they are doing it to save other Leahs. There's no reason to feel left out. There's more reason to feel 'My God, what a good mother and father I've got, they're saving children's lives'.

I pray to Leah every night. After Dad tucks me in I pray to God and Jesus and say Amen to them. Then I pray to my Nan and Leah.

Leah, aged three, at Essex Marina on the river Crouch.

Cindy and Leah, 1982.

Our wedding, 25 September 1982. Emily, Cindy, Leah and Wendy as bridesmaids.

William's christening. Left to right: Emily, Paul, Janet and William, Cindy, Wendy and Leah.

Leah dressed up as Father Christmas.

Leah aged 10.

Easter 1993. Leah, aged 15, Paul and William at the river Stour.

Leah aged 16, March 1994.

Happy times . . . Leah (centre) is pictured with friends Louise and Lee at a college social event.

Leah (left) and Sarah on the night of the party.

The last picture of Leah, taken moments before she died.

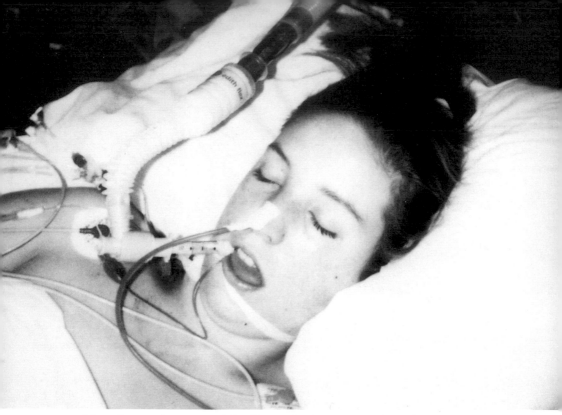

The picture that started it all . . . Leah connected to the ventilator at Broomfield Hospital, November 1995.

November 16, 1995, just four hours after Leah's life-support machine was switched off, we faced a press conference at the hospital.
(*Essex Chronicle*)

Don officiated at Leah's funeral and leads the way as her coffin is carried from the church. (*Essex Chronicle*)

'I Will Always Love You' – the theme tune from the film *The Bodyguard* which we were watching on Leah's party night – seemed an appropriate message.

William's touching farewell to Leah.

I feel like Leah is still with us. If I want someone to talk to, I talk to Leah. I thought she looked so nice in her party clothes, and so did some of the boys who came to the party! I imagine her in those clothes. It's like playing cowboys and indians on your own. You have to imagine, if you are the cowboy, the indian in front of you. It's like that for me with Leah.

I believe Leah really is there. Not like a ghost that comes back to haunt you, but exactly the same as she was in real life, it's just that I can't touch her.

JANET: Part of William's childhood died the day Leah took that fateful Ecstasy tablet. He has witnessed some very distressing scenes, at close quarters, scenes that youngsters of his age are rarely exposed to. As a result, he has had to cope with some difficult emotions in his formative years. To repeat his quote in the introduction to this book: 'When people take drugs it only affects their bodies, doesn't it? But when they become ill, or die, it affects everyone.' What a profound statement from one so young – and how true it is!

6

A Time for Action

JANET: We have already touched on our trip to Liverpool, the day after Leah's death, to appear on the *This Morning* programme. The day proved to be a very significant one for Paul and me, not just because it prompted the idea of the *Sorted* video, but because it was the day we realised we could actually do something positive about what had happened to Leah. At the same time, it changed the course of our lives.

Jason, the researcher of the programme, met us at Abridge airfield in the morning. The television company had its own private plane. Cindy and her boyfriend Greg, Wendy and Norman, and Emily and her friend Jennifer travelled to Liverpool as well.

I have a fear of flying. I had expected to see something like a jumbo jet, but, this was just a tiny six-seater. 'Oh no,' I thought, 'I can't get on that plane – no way.'

In the meantime, Andy Hamill, who was back at our home, had telephoned our local radio station, BBC Essex. He told them we were on our way to the airfield, and would they play 'I Will Always Love You' by Whitney Houston for us. Music is not normally played on the morning programme, but Shaun Peel, the presenter, made an exception just for us. He played the record, at 7.30am, in memory of Leah, the exact moment we were about to get out of the car. I'm sure hearing that record was what enabled me to get on the plane.

As the plane left the ground I can remember saying the Lord's Prayer to myself, I was so frightened. I was looking out of the window at the scenery down below through the clouds. It was a clear day. Then Paul looked at me and said: 'Do you realise, Leah can see this all the time now?' It made me cry.

Cindy and Greg travelled separately, from Stansted airport, as our plane was not large enough to accommodate everyone. When we all eventually arrived at the television studios, it was interesting to see in actuality all the things we had seen before on our television. Just after the news, Wendy, Cindy, Emily, Paul and I were taken down to be met by the presenters, Richard Madeley and Judy Finnegan. The set always looks big on TV but, in reality, it was actually quite small. The chef was there to do his piece. He had four or five 'slaves' dashing about helping to prepare things for him off-set.

Richard and Judy were very nice, even empathetic. They told us they had 18-year-old twins at university and that they too had worried about what their children might be getting up to. We were just one set of parents talking to another. They were genuinely concerned. The interview went quite well, and then the girls came on. Afterwards, the telephones went wild – scores of people were ringing in. And so the *Sorted* video idea was born.

Before we left the studio, Jason told us the producer of *World in Action* wanted to see us. The producer arrived and expressed an interest in following up the interview with a programme. Then somebody rang up from the Central Television studios in Birmingham. Would we go to Birmingham that night to appear on their programme *Live*? Jason advised caution. He suggested we do it if we wanted to, but warned that it might be a bit of a bear pit.

Paul spoke to the man on the telephone. They wanted us to appear on the programme, face to face, with some drug dealers. Paul said 'No, I couldn't do that, not at the moment. The way I feel right now, I'd floor them.' 'OK', came the reply, 'we'll get back to you.' They did. 'Would we be prepared to appear on the programme if we were in a separate room from the dealers?' Paul agreed. It was arranged to take the whole family to an hotel in Birmingham where we could all have a meal, paid for by the television company, and have time to relax before appearing on the programme in the evening. Then they telephoned us again. The dealers, they said, had refused to go into a separate room, but they had agreed to go behind a darkened screen. We agreed and travelled to Birmingham.

By the time we arrived at the hotel, we were all very tired. The television company had arranged for us to have three or four rooms between us. We had a short rest before gathering together in the dining room. We all sat there together, with a posh menu in front of us. The manager came up to us and said we could have whatever we wanted, Central Television would pay, but none of us were hungry.

Paul has since said he felt so guilty. There we were, being treated like royalty, and the only reason we were there was because of the death of his daughter. 'The cheapest thing on the menu is about £15,' he said. 'I can't justify this.' While we were in the dining room, Jason telephoned to let us know that British Telecom wanted to produce a video as a result of the massive response to our interview in the morning.

At last we arrived at the *Live* studio. We didn't know quite what to expect. Our only previous similar experience had been the night before in Norwich, but to be honest, we had been almost out of it then through sheer exhaustion.

We were told our family would be sitting in the front row, with Paul and me just in front of them. It was then they told us the pushers would also be out the front but that they were now refusing to go behind a screen. By this time, we were being filmed behind the scenes, so there wasn't an awful lot we could do about it. We felt we had been set up.

Nicky Campbell was one of the presenters, Adrian Mills the other. They were very nice. Adrian, in fact, burst into tears when he first shook our hands. 'Don't worry,' they told us. 'We know you're not professionals at this kind of thing. We'll walk out, the audience will clap, and you'll see your chairs in front of you. Just sit down and we'll start the programme.'

We walked out, hand in hand. In front of us, right out in front of everyone, were two *Mastermind* type chairs so far apart, we couldn't even reach each other for comfort. I took one look and thought 'Oh my God!' I felt numb.

Then the pushers came on, one girl and five lads. They were in disguise, wearing balaclavas and dark glasses. They sprawled across their chairs and adopted an arrogant pose for the cameras. Upset as I was, I was determined not to give those people the satisfaction of seeing me cry or lose my temper. I thought they were scum, they were just not worth it.

One of them had a little daughter of two years. A member of the audience called out to him 'Would you let your daughter take it?' 'No, I wouldn't,' he replied. 'I'm a good parent.' The audience went wild. Ecstasy victim Daniel Ashton's mum was also in the studio with other members of his family. In fact, Daniel's brother got so angry he had to leave the set. Another woman in the audience called out to one of the dealers, 'I suppose you're going out after the show to sell some more!' He replied: 'I've got some on me now, dear, how many do you want?'

At one point in the programme, one of the pushers kept calling me 'luvvie'. Paul was going purple with rage and began to rise from his chair. I think Paul almost felt like killing him. Fortunately, Norman was behind him to push him back down.

After the programme, we went into a cloakroom to be reunited with our family before going to the hospitality room. The girls were crying and Paul was very close to tears. Although I had managed not to cry on camera, when I got into the room I just burst into tears. As I have already said, Cindy is not one to normally show her emotions, but the experience of seeing the attitudes of the pushers at close quarters had absolutely enraged her. 'Mum,' she said, 'may I swear?'

'Cindy, please go ahead,' I replied, 'because that's exactly how I feel.'

'Those blokes are f***ing ars*h*les!' she said. I had to agree.

It was then that one lad, a drug user, came up to us and said, 'Never, ever again will I take Ecstasy. I didn't know what I was doing. No one told me how dangerous it was. I thought I was just having a good time. I won't touch the stuff any more.' Paul and I looked at each other. We realised that his response, if nothing else, had made our journey worthwhile. That's when the idea of carrying on our message began to take shape. We were taken home in a minibus, arriving, tired out, at about 3am.

Our experience in Liverpool made us aware of several things. We realised many youngsters, like their mates, were buying drugs from dealers who were saying things like, 'It's good stuff, you'll have a great time on this.' Nobody, it seemed was saying 'Do you know what this can really do to you?' I don't think recreational drugs were talked about so openly at the time.

Not many people seemed to know much about that type of drug culture, and that included us. The only reason we had been on the programme was because we were bereaved parents. We were sure there was much more to the drug scene than we realised. But it was obvious that the public had not been sufficiently educated about drugs, and we resolved to do something about it. In fact, when *Sorted* was about to be released to schools, representatives of the government asked for it to be put on hold for six months.

The government was developing a drugs strategy and parents' guide which was not yet up to date. They didn't want us to beat them to it. The Granada Television researchers refused to delay the release – and within a week, the Prime Minister, John Major, announced a grant of £15m to the Health Education Authority to create the National Drugs Line and Parents' Guide. We're not saying *Sorted* prompted that response, but we certainly think its release moved things on by a minimum of three months.

When Leah was in hospital, many people had offered help, including money. We decided to launch Leah's Appeal to raise money for the hospital. A man, Peter Shipton, from our village, sold his house and gave us £250. 'Something has got to be done,' he said. The Metropolitan Police collected fingerprints of famous people and auctioned them off. After a while, the money began to build up.

Stephanie Martin, the PR woman at the hospital, told us that for a mobile ventilator, a bed and a heater, we would need to raise about

£10,200. We decided to go for it.

Just before Christmas, Paul received a telephone call from a man called Steve Mervish. He told us about the work of an orthodox Jewish rabbi, Rabbi Saffrin, who runs the Drugs Chabad in Ilford, Essex. Rabbi Saffrin had become involved with working with young people and had started his own sort of drugs-awareness campaign. He would talk to them, advise them, and he ran a helpline.

Steve asked Paul if they could visit us. Paul agreed. Rabbi Saffrin told us more about his work and offered to help us in any way he could. He told us about his school in Barkingside. The parents of the children, he said, were mostly very wealthy and he could talk to them until he was blue in the face about the dangers of drugs but they didn't seem to take much notice of him.

Rabbi Saffrin invited us to be guest speakers at a Sixties Night he had arranged at the school. Would we be prepared to talk about our experiences? Although we had never done anything like this before, we agreed to come along. Paul's philosophy in life is that if you fail to prepare, you prepare to fail, so he set about working on our speech.

When we arrived at the school hall, we were aware of people staring at us. It was as if they had seen our faces somewhere before but didn't yet realise who we were. We sat down at the top table with Steve and his wife, among others. They were very nice. There was no alcohol at all, just soft drinks and a big buffet, which was absolutely incredible. I did the raffle. There were some fantastic prizes, donated by the wealthy parents – things like stereos and televisions. After the food, Rabbi Saffrin stood up and gave an introduction about his work with Drugs Chabad. The idea of the evening was to raise money for his campaign. Then he introduced us.

Paul stood up and gave what he now describes as our experience. He gave a short introduction to Leah's life, what we thought we had done to make her aware of the dangers of drugs, what happened at the party, and how Leah had ended up. At the end, Paul was virtually in tears. He told them their kids all still had a chance and wished everyone a long and happy life. As he got down, the audience gave him a standing ovation and the money began flowing from left, right and centre into the Rabbi's appeal. Paul just fell into my arms, crying his eyes out and, I noticed, many of the audience were crying too.

Because it was a Sixties Night, there was a live band with a girl singer, who I can only describe as a Lulu double. She was absolutely brilliant. It was our era of music and, eventually, we got up to have a dance with everyone else. It was only then we realised how guilty we felt. There we were, enjoying a dance, but Leah was dead.

Some time later, we were in Amsterdam with a *World in Action* production team. We had done quite a bit of work with this crew over the previous three weeks and had built up a good rapport with them. We had become friends. The producer, Sarah, said on the last night there, 'Let's go out and have a meal.' We found a little restaurant that served up some lovely food and we had a pleasant evening with which came a welcome release of tension after a traumatic three weeks of filming. Something made us all start to laugh. All the camera crew and production people, like us, were laughing and giggling like a bunch of silly schoolkids. Once again though, we felt so very, very guilty that we had been able to enjoy ourselves.

Even today those guilt feelings recur now and then. A year or so after Leah's death they prompted us to have a talk with Don. He reminded us that life is for the living. Leah is dead, he said. We would never forget her or get over her death, but we had to learn to live without her. He told us we still had William, Wendy, Cindy and Emily, and each other. Life must go on – until that big day when we all would meet again.

The success of Paul's talk at the school further emphasised to us the power of the message we could deliver to those prepared to listen. We had to go on. We felt there was a desperate need for more talks just like it. Many parents, it seemed, were quite unaware of the size and growth of the recreational drugs culture.

7

Sisterly Love

JANET: Life experience is valuable to everyone. It provides the blocks with which we build the foundation of our life's ambitions and begins the moulding of what we would like to achieve in life. The experience of Leah's death affected Wendy, Cindy and Emily in different ways and, with their help, we want to describe how they have coped with their emotions.

Wendy had always been a good listener and counsellor. She trained as a nurse, her speciality being mental health. Her partner, Norman, lectures and counsels in the same field.

His words to us after Leah's death were: 'I've worked in the field of bereavement counselling for years now, but however much you can counsel other people, it doesn't help you personally when you go through it. You've no idea what it's like until you've experienced it.'

I think those words probably say it all for Wendy. She has gone through a traumatic but valuable experience. She still gets bad days. Like us, she and Norman have had to rely on each other for support, and this has reinforced their relationship in a world where not everything is romance and roses.

Wendy is in a career where many of her clients are doing drugs. Reading about the damaging effects of drug abuse in textbooks is no substitute for personal experience. For her, there is no glamour in the drugs scene – she sees the true effects every day. She has learnt a new aspect of caring.

Emily has always been an independent little fighter. She worked hard to get her BA, the last year of which was interrupted by Leah's death. She has always expressed herself strongly about the stupidity of drug-taking, a view powerfully reinforced by what happened to Leah.

It took Emily several attempts to pick up her social life immediately afterwards, and she was lucky she had some very good friends to see her through, in the forms of Jenny and Emma. This was just as well, for on one of her first outings with her friends to their usual pub at Christmas 1995, a lad came up and asked her if she wanted to buy some stuff. She froze, stared him out and, such was the venom in that stare, one of her friends, worried that Emily might hit him, said: 'I think you'd better just GO AWAY!' He did.

Emily will be able to pass on the essence of this personal experience to her charges in her teaching profession, and push for more honesty and reality in drug awareness.

Cindy is outwardly the strongest character of all the girls but, in a lot of ways, she is the softest. She sometimes finds it hard to show emotion and would more readily cry with anger than with sorrow, as she showed in her reaction to the pushers at Central Television. She too, was lucky to have the support of her boyfriend, Greg, and his family.

Cindy is studying in a university town known for its drug taking. It sounds a strange thing to say, but Cindy always benefits the most by learning the hard way and, in the field of drugs, she certainly did that, with Leah's experience.

Cindy freely admits she will go to the pub and get tiddly, but I would rather she did that than take drugs like Ecstasy. At least alcohol and its effects are known quantities, and, if she feels a need to conform to student ways of recreation, then let it be that. However, she is a deep thinker, and no one will make her do anything against her will.

In many ways, Cindy and Leah were alike. I often ask Cindy's advice on drug matters and seek her reactions to different ideas people come up with. She answers honestly, and will still say to me: 'You don't still have to ask me if I'm doing it, do you mum?'

But she knows why I ask. I am still fearful for her.

All three girls have recorded their individual memories of Leah and what happened to her.

WENDY: When we were young, Leah and I spent most weekends together. We used to go to ballet classes together. We had a close relationship, a sort of big sister, little sister relationship, as I was five years older than her.

We used to talk to each other a lot, especially when Dot, her mother, died. She was very confused at the time. Dot's death hit her very badly. I hope I was able to reassure her and I think it helped her to discuss what had happened to her mother.

I can't remember ever talking to Leah about drugs or anything like that, but I can't say I was really surprised when I heard that she had taken an Ecstasy tablet – it's something so many youngsters these days seem to be doing. Leah's friends didn't seem particularly wild. They were rather quiet actually – compared to Leah! She was very outgoing, a bubbly person – a typical teenager, I suppose.

I am a mental-health nurse and, on the night of Leah's party, I was on night duty. When my partner Norman telephoned me so late at night, I guessed straight away that something was wrong. You don't often get telephone calls at that hour. 'There's been an accident,' he said. 'Leah's taken an overdose.'

We didn't realise at the time she had taken an Ecstasy tablet. In fact, I assumed he meant she had taken something like paracetamol. Nevertheless, when I put the telephone down I was very shocked. I sat down and waited for Norman to arrive. I was quite shaky and began to cry. One of my colleagues tried to reassure me that Leah would be all right. 'They'll pump her out, and she'll be fine,' she said.

The thought crossed my mind that, when Leah recovered, she would need counselling and I hoped she wouldn't require appointments in the department where I worked. It's funny how many silly thoughts race through your head at such times.

Although Leah was brought to Broomfield Hospital, where I work, it is a large facility and the accident and emergency department was some distance from where I was based. Norman arrived, with William, to pick me up to take me there.

On the way, William was in a state of shock. He was rambling, going on about the police coming to the house and he was very confused. He didn't really seem to understand what was going on. He told me that Mum and Dad had been giving Leah the kiss of life. That's when I began to realise how serious the situation was.

When we arrived at the accident and emergency department, Mum and Dad were waiting in a side room. They were in a state of shock. They told me about the Ecstasy, but I can't really remember my reaction to the news. Everything at that particular stage is now a blur to me.

I didn't see Leah that night. She was in the resuscitation room, so I sat with Mum and Dad for a few minutes. William was waiting outside in the car so, after a while, Norman and I left to take him back to our home, which is near the hospital. William was by now completely shattered, so we put him to bed and we stayed up for the rest of the night talking about what had happened.

We returned to the hospital at 9am. We went through to the intensive care unit to see Leah. It was a terrible shock to see her all wired up. That's when the reality of the situation finally dawned on me.

Over the next few days, our home became a guest-house for the rest of the family, somewhere to meet up before and after visits to Leah's bedside. I think the experience of those few days brought out the practical side of me.

As time went on, I realised it would be unlikely that Leah would recover. The nurses were warning us of possible bad news and I began to lose hope. I remember sitting with Leah, talking to her and willing her to come round We played her favourite music and so on but, after a few days, it began to sink in: Leah was not going to recover.

This was confirmed when the family were gathered together in a waiting room and a doctor came in to break the news to us. I had been expecting it, but it was still a shock. I had a feeling of total helplessness. This couldn't really be happening, I thought. I'll wake up in a moment and it will all have been a bad dream.

I was very surprised at the media attention over Leah. You sometimes see these things on television but you never really expect anything like that to happen in your own family, do you?

There is not a day that goes by when I do not think about Leah and often, it gets to me. She was just a normal teenager, doing what many teenagers do. It's just that, in Leah's case, it blew up in her face.

CINDY: We were much the same age, more friends than sisters. When we were younger, we often had rows because we wanted each other's things and so on. We had good times as well, though. I remember the times we had on Dad's boat. Leah and I shared a cabin and we used to play this stupid game of lying in our beds with our feet in the air, singing stupid songs. One of our favourite television programmes was *3-2-1* with Ted Rogers, and we used to enjoy watching it together.

We got on much better when we were older, in fact there were times when we were like the best of mates. As teenagers – I suppose we were 17 or 18 – we would occasionally go out to a nightclub together and have a good time.

I knew only a few of Leah's friends. They were much like my own. Being at university myself, I know of several friends who are doing recreational drugs. Most teenagers would know someone. I didn't know Leah was dabbling in drugs but, because of the clubs she went to and some of the people she knew, I had an inkling that, if she was going to do them herself, it would most likely be at one of the clubs we went to, or with the friends she hung around with.

I have never tried any drugs – I've never wanted to. It's not very nice to see one of your friends 'off their face', is it? I don't even smoke, although several of my friends do.

It was on the Sunday morning after Leah's party when I first heard what had happened to her. I was in Sheffield, where I was studying. My boyfriend Greg was downstairs. He had been ill and so he was staying with me. I was upstairs when the telephone rang, I ran downstairs to answer it. It was Emily. 'Leah took a tablet at her party. They've taken her to hospital, but it doesn't look good. Can you come down? Mum wants to see you.'

I was so shocked, I had to sit down. I burst out crying. Greg and I got the train to Essex. The journey seemed to take ages. Wendy picked us up at Chelmsford station. At first, I didn't want to go in to see Leah. I was too scared. William told me I should see her. It was horrible. It is so hard to talk to someone all the time not knowing if they can hear you or not.

After Leah died, Greg and I went to see her in the chapel of rest. It was awful. I just glanced at her and came straight out again. I would have preferred to have remembered her as she was when she was healthy. As for the funeral service, it was almost unreal. There were so many cameras there.

I was worried about how people at the university would react towards me. Everyone knew what had happened because of all the publicity in the newspapers and on the television. I need not have worried. People tried not to mention it too much and only my close friends talked to me about Leah. In the main, most people tried to talk to me as they would normally.

Because I am stuck up in Sheffield, miles away from Mum, I am not so involved in what she and Dad are trying to do. But it seems strange sometimes, to pick up a music magazine to find an article about drugs with a picture of them next to it, or to turn on the television and suddenly see them.

I think Leah's death hit Wendy and Emily more than it hit me. After all, she was their little sister. We were more like friends – but, of course, I do miss her. It's not so bad when I am up in Sheffield but, when I come home, I really notice the fact she is not there any more. That's when I really start to think how much damage just one little pill can cause. It's hard to believe, isn't it? £10 – that's all it takes to kill someone.

EMILY: Every summer Mum and Dad used to take us in the boat to Althorne, near Maldon. We had some good times there at weekends. Leah and I enjoyed a very close relationship – she and I were the 'feminine' ones, messing around with make-up, while Wendy and Cindy were more like tomboys, going out on their bikes.

I hate the term 'step-sister'. Leah was my *sister*. I suppose we would have spoken about drugs at some time – doesn't everyone when the subject comes up on the news or times like that? However, until Leah became ill I was as naïve as anyone could be on the subject. I knew drugs like heroin were really dangerous but, on the other hand, I knew thousands of kids went out each week-end to use recreational drugs. Looking back, I suppose I should have known that Leah might have tried some herself. After all, she went to nightclubs.

I've been to clubs myself, but I was never into the drug culture, although I have been approached in clubs and asked if I was 'sorted' – a reference to Ecstasy. I always just turned away. I have never been curious enough to want to try it, although I've got friends who have. I always thought it was a certain kind of person that took drugs, not someone like Leah.

I had, in fact, been out to a club on the night of Leah's party and I did not get back until the early hours. I was living with my grand-mother in Dagenham at the time. She came in to tell me Mum had telephoned to let us know that Leah was in hospital. She'd taken an overdose.

I couldn't understand why Leah would take an overdose on the night of her party. It just didn't add up. When I questioned my grandmother more, she told me Leah had taken an Ecstasy tablet. I just assumed she was suffering from dehydration and didn't think the situation was all that serious. Nevertheless, I hurried to get ready to go to the hospital. A friend gave me a lift. Although I didn't expect Leah's condition to be at all life-threatening, I can remember crying on the way.

When I arrived I saw Wendy. She looked very tearful and I realised then that things were probably more serious than I had imagined. Mum and Dad came out to the side room to meet me. They were in quite a state. They told me Leah was in a coma and on a life support machine. I asked if I could see her and Dad took me in. It really hit me hard to see her like that.

I visited Leah each day while she was in the hospital. I would arrive about 6am and stay until about 11pm, spending the time playing music to her, massaging her hands and feet and talking about anything I could think of, like what had been happening on *EastEnders*, silly things like that.

In the back of my mind, I think I knew Leah's machine would eventually have to be turned off, but, while her chest was still going up and down and she remained warm, I just couldn't give up any hope. It was a terrible shock though, when the doctors told us Leah was clinically dead. We all just tried to comfort each other.

When, at first, I heard there was to be a story about Leah in the newspaper, I assumed it would be in our local newspaper, but she was in all the nationals and, the morning after her party, she was featured on *The Big Breakfast* television news programme. I thought, 'Oh my God! I can't believe it', and then a couple of my friends telephoned to say they had seen my sister on the news.

It is only when I look back now that I realise how public Leah's death was. Sometimes I wish it hadn't been so, but I can see why Mum and Dad made their decision to bring everything out into the open. They didn't want Leah to die and that be it. Just the same, at Leah's funeral, when I saw all the cameras, my first thought was 'Go away and leave us alone, we don't need you today.'

Leah's death has made me realise I am not immortal. I think about her a lot and I miss her very much. Leah had her whole life ahead of her. She was only 18 and was hoping to teach and go around the world with her friend Sarah.

One tablet was all it took to end all those dreams.

8

Journeys of Discovery

JANET: One of the most significant programmes in which we have taken part, and to which we really owe the start of our 'education' into the drug world, was *World in Action*. We had been approached by one of the production team while we were up in Liverpool on *This Morning*, and we agreed that they should send a producer to discuss the programme with us.

The lady they sent was Sarah Mainwaring-White, a petite blonde, who Paul instantly fancied, and I instantly envied, but we all made friends immediately. I was worried what to have for lunch, as none of us had eaten, and I thought such a well-spoken lady would want posh nosh. Not a bit of it! She positively drooled when Paul offered baked beans and free-range home-grown eggs. It was one of those meals that you always remember.

Sarah outlined what she thought we might do in the programme, the people she wanted us to meet, and the places she wanted us to go. More importantly, she had a genuine empathy. We not only chatted about the programme, but other things as well – our family, her friends – and we knew we would feel comfortable with her. We have learned this is very important when putting your all into a programme. You need to be able to trust those making it. Just like Sue Durkan, the producer of *Sorted*, Sarah knew exactly what she wanted to do.

The idea was to take us on a journey – a journey to see what was going on in the recreational drug scene and how different agencies were dealing with it at the time. It was calculated that filming would take two to three weeks, with Christmas in between.

Bear in mind that many hours of filming were done for this 25-minute programme. A lot of information we collected did not make it on to the television screen. For that reason, we want to outline that information here, because the experience opened up an unknown world to us.

The crew consisted of George Jesse Turner, the cameraman, who as far as seeing life is concerned has been there, done it and bought the T-shirt; Keith Staniforth, the technical assistant; and Mark Atkinson, the sound man. Duncan Staff was the assistant producer/drug-buyer lookalike. The first place we visited was Manchester Royal Infirmary, to talk with a Dr Morton, the accident and emergency consultant. She was a concerned parent herself, and became even more worried by the number of drug-related casualties on checking the record for the previous six months. She found 47 patients in those months who had admitted they had a problem with Ecstasy, and these were young people in their teens or early twenties who had taken only one or two tablets.

Dr Morton told us that what terrified her was the uncertainty regarding the effect of Ecstasy. If you take 20 aspirin tablets you expect to be ill, but one won't hurt you, yet one or two Ecstasy tablets can give you a buzz – or they can kill you . . .

These were only 'E' casualties, but she had also counted numerous attendencies suffering from the effects of speed, heroin, or cannabis. With an unexpected death, she explained, the coroner will usually record only the final cause of death – liver or kidney failure, for instance, and will be reluctant to put precipitating factors, such as the effects of drugs, because the next of kin have to live with the stigma of a drug-related death for the rest of their lives.

While in Manchester, we visited Debbie Warburton's family. Debbie became ill in 1991, and died in 1992. Her death was recorded as liver failure, caused by months of taking Ecstasy. She had kept diaries of her drug-taking habits, charting all the times it made her ill, as well as the highs. She tells of the feeling she got when she took her first tablet, and how she chased that feeling forever afterwards, increasing her dose until it quadrupled. Then she became ill, and could not face any more. Yet she was compelled to go back. The depressions and paranoia set in, and her personality changed. She had even taken part in the making of a video singing the drug's praises. She never saw the video go out on television because she died, after 10 days in a coma.

Listening to her on the video was almost like listening to someone describing a religious cult. Her family were, and still are, determined to highlight the dangers of Ecstasy use. Like us, the wider effects on the family have taken their toll, but they have come through and are still campaigning.

Margaret Keighly-Bray (Debbie's mother) was a primary-school teacher for 28 years, and says drug awareness should start there. 'We underestimate our 10- and 11-year-olds,' she said, 'and they copy their older brothers and sisters.' Meeting them made us realise we were not alone in this fight. They represented for us all the people who had contacted us, and could truly empathise with us.

The place many people go to for information and advice on drugs in the Manchester area is the organisation Lifeline. They try to take a middle-of-the-road approach, appreciating many recreational drug users do not see it as a problem at first, but will get in trouble a few months down the line, and then they are there for them. They pride themselves that they do not lecture, but tell the truth about the effects of drugs, be they good or bad.

Talking to Alan and Ian at Lifeline, it was clear to us that there were many unanswered questions about recreational drugs, Ecstasy in particular. They had been seeing Ecstasy casualties in their work since 1988, when they were working in Newham, London – not just deaths, but psychiatric casualties. In 1991 they were invited to a conference in Barcelona, where they had related their experiences to researchers, doctors and others, and these experts had flatly refused to concede that Ecstasy could ever be problematic. They were talking then not of deaths, but of a whole range of behavioural problems.

Like us, the Lifeline staff were concerned by the huge gap between drugs education in schools, on the one hand, and, on the other hand, the range of treatment services that exist predominantly for people who are injecting heroin, most of whom first report for treatment in their twenties.

There is a hiatus, in terms of treatment centres and facilities, between those available for addicts in their twenties or older, and children of 14 or 15 years of age, which is when most youngsters start experimenting with recreational drugs. That is the gap Lifeline has tried to fill. They also run Parentline, which is open four evenings a week because of the demand. They try to match a parent who has a particular problem face-to-face with someone who has had a similar problem. They will also see the users themselves, with their parents where possible.

What they had noticed was that, although the main body of people contacting them were families with a user on heroin or cocaine, the number on Ecstasy and amphetamines was on the increase. It made us determined to help fill the gap if we possibly could and helped shape the character of our organisation Action for Drug Awareness (ADA), particularly as far as parents were concerned.

Paul also visited Manchester Police to meet DCI Postles, who is in charge of the drug squad, and Alan Castree, the Assistant Chief Constable. The essence of what they said to him was that a multi-disciplinary approach is needed to combat this problem. The DAT (Drug Action Teams) were just beginning to come together.

Our next visit took us to see Karl Jansen, a psychiatrist at the Maudsley Hospital in London. He seemed in no doubt that Ecstasy was neurotoxic – that is destructively poisonous to the nervous system – but that the doses and frequency of use necessary to cause such damage seemed to have a question mark over them.

What he *did* say, which we found very interesting, was that if you need to take an increasingly larger dose in order to get the same feeling again as with your first tablet, then it is quite likely that you have already suffered damaging changes in your brain, and that is why you are not getting the high any more.

He believes that Ecstasy punches a hole between your conscious and subconscious, the stuff that nightmares and psychoses are made of, and that without the psychotherapeutic back-up which the drug was originally intended to be used with, it could have very unpleasant consequences. His other concern was that all the tests done so far were either on squirrel monkeys' brains, which are less sensitive to substances than human brains, and that experiments done thus far with human guinea pigs are under the kind of strictly controlled conditions which would be found within the framework of the drug's original psychotherapeutic use.

In Karl's opinion the worst possible place to take Ecstasy is in a club setting. No research has been done into the effects of Ecstasy in this setting, particularly in the doses now regarded as the norm for clubbers. He also agreed with us that accurate figures for the total number of Ecstasy casualties – not just deaths – were not available, and that while the figure of 50 deaths was being banded around, the people holding the purse-strings for research fellowships had failed to see the importance of such work until recently. However, in 1997, Karl was granted funding to take his research further, as was Dr John Henry at Guy's Hospital, London.

A lot of dialogue between Paul and me was recorded, and right through was the message that youngsters needed to be told the whole truth. But what is the whole truth? The fact is, not enough is known about Ecstasy – and that, in itself, is dangerous.

We talked of all the letters we had received, many of them from parents of Ecstasy casualties, all backing up the concerns we already had. We were also learning of some of the charming tactics dealers were using. These cuddly, caring 'friends' of clubbers were giving out the first pill free, then approaching the now high clubber and saying, 'Great feeling, isn't it? Want to buy another?', or dropping one in someone's drink so they could sample the experience. Anything to sell the stuff.

Some bouncers were taking the stuff off customers at the door and then re-selling it inside, or they would give clubbers the choice: 'Either give it to us, or we call the law', thus endearing themselves to the local constabulary for being watchful door staff, or making money from the gear. Either way, they could not lose.

Bear in mind that, at the time, we were just like many parents still are – we were green as grass. We could not believe this was really going on in good old law-abiding Britain. As far as I was concerned, this only happened in American movies. Paul had a bit more insight, because of his police experience, but even he was astounded at the escalation of it.

Our journey across to Amsterdam was preceded by a visit to Customs & Excise to meet Dick Brown, deputy head of investigations at Custom House. What an amazing and beautifully historic building Custom House is. It is tall, strong, and impressive, and in the middle of all this we sat with Dick at a coffee table, on which were five large plastic bags of Ecstasy tablets: 30 kilos, 3,000 to 5,000 tablets, worth about £2m.

In such a setting you almost expected the old time smuggler with the parrot on his shoulder to be dragged before you, kicking and cursing. Nothing so simple. These drugs were smuggled through in a calculated, clever way, born of an ever more mechanised age. These bags were one hit, imported from the Netherlands. The feeling I had looking at those tablets overwhelmed me, and I became choked up. It was like wartime bombs, whose name was on the next one?

Dick showed us photographs of some of the places people hide drugs to smuggle them through. You need imagination to think some of them up and, as Dick said, 'The best detective has a criminal mind, not a criminal mentality.'

Largely due to the work of our British Customs, the dealers have had to import the stuff as more British 'factories' have been found and disposed of. They have an incredible task to do in Customs & Excise. When you consider that 43 million people pass through Heathrow Airport each year alone, how on earth they do as much as they do is quite remarkable. Their resources have been cut, but still they are dedicated to keeping on top of things. I have great admiration for them, and we should all continue to assist them, through intelligence, like Crimestoppers, and our judiciary should back them when they are successful.

On our way out from Heathrow Airport, we stopped to look at how the Customs officers work. We could see the magnitude of the problems Dick Brown had described, and we saw it on a quiet day! Seeing the interview rooms behind the scenes was enough to put anyone off wanting to end up in one. They were so stark, and the 'special' loos were definitely enough to deter anyone thinking of hiding the stuff more imaginatively, let alone anyone thinking of becoming a Customs officer! The word 'search' took on a whole new meaning!

When we arrived in the Netherlands, we met Superintendent Bernard Scholten of the Amsterdam police. He attempted to explain the situation in Holland, which includes a fairly draconian law based on the Opium Act, coupled with a remarkably liberal acceptance of drug taking. Some of their ideas seemed very positive, like 11- and 12-year-olds being taken to police stations to talk to heroin addicts to hear from the horse's mouth what it is like to be enslaved by the drug.

Other ideas seemed strange to us like police attending house parties to keep an eye on conditions there, while turning a blind eye to the possession of drugs for personal use. Thirty grams of cannabis is allowed, or half a gram of what they define as hard drugs, like heroin, cocaine and Ecstasy. Deaths and casualties do occur, and when they do they try to find out why.

Their Opium Act says drugs are illegal, and according to this law, you should not even be able to buy cannabis in coffee shops, but they made the 'blind eye' decision because their detention facilities could not cope with the number of users. Moreover, they realised that while they were spending so much time on the users, the big drug-trafficking cartels at the top were being ignored.

It is a difficult balance to strike, Bernard Scholten agrees, and he was not suggesting they have got it right in Holland by any means. What he did say was that he thinks Holland has gained its reputation for drug supply because people wishing to use drugs can buy them far more easily there than in countries like the UK.

But this does not mean, he explained, that the Dutch police are not vigilant in trying to stamp out drugs, it is just that their priorities are different from our policing system. They have a hard core of 500 or so hard-drug users. If one of those is arrested for the fourth time in any 12 months, the addict has to make a decision – gaol, or a clinic for treatment.

The police also crack down on any addict causing a problem in the local community. Ecstasy, however, is becoming a problem in Amsterdam, and he seemed uncertain as to how they would handle it.

We visited one of the coffee shops and watched as a young man showed us how to roll a joint. Paul put it to him that in the UK he could have been arrested for that, which the young man found strange for, as far as he was concerned, cannabis was 'unbelievably harmless' because 'it grows all over the world'.

The girl behind the counter showed us a 'menu' of all the leaf cannabis and resins available, and even offered a cannabis cake. Be warned – if you visit Holland, you do not go into a coffee shop for coffee and cakes in the conventional sense.

We talked to the shop owner, Rayer Elzinga, of the union of coffee shop owners. He had been to a meeting in The Hague, where it was proposed to cut the allowed amount of cannabis for sale to each customer from 30 to five grams. Not surprisingly, he was not happy with this idea. Rayer buys all his cannabis from a source which he has known for years. As he put it, because he sells it in his own shop, 'they [the police] know when they stop me that I pay tax and that when they catch two or three kilos on me, I put it on my tax bill – and that is a legal thing.'

As far as he was concerned, cannabis is totally harmless, non-addictive, and does not lead to the use of harder drugs. Alcohol and tobacco he sees as problematical drugs. He even claimed if you went into a café where they were smoking cannabis and drinking alcohol as well, that there was less trouble from the alcohol.

This is a dubious message. Even the Dutch government will close down any coffee shop selling the two together, with no arguments, and they now acknowledge that they have a big problem with people dependent on cannabis.

I began to feel this was a question of which culture you were brought up in, and was certainly not convinced that the coffee shop set-up could stand serious examination. My observations of people leaving the coffee shops, and climbing on to their bicycles or into their cars in a very dubious state, reminded me of some of the less salubrious pubs back home at turning-out time before the drink-driving laws were enacted.

One day, crossing a bridge in Amsterdam where dealers were hanging out, we decided to go for a walk on our own while the crew were filming. We discovered, quite by accident, the city's cannabis museum. I learned a lot in there about the original uses of hemp. It is indeed a pity that such a useful substance has become yet another money-making street drug. In the museum you could buy everything needed to grow and process cannabis. It was just like a garden centre for hashish. They were even growing it hydroponically, under lights.

Sarah got permission to film in there. When we went into the growing room, Paul said: 'Blimey, it smells like cat's wee.' I elbowed him. 'For God's sake, don't put that in the programme,' I said to Sarah, and what does she do? She puts it in! It did pong, though, and it *was* like cat's wee.

In Amsterdam it is possible to get the drugs you are going to buy, or deal, tested. It was put to us in the UK that this was the answer to all Ecstasy casualties, the reasoning being that it is not the drug itself that does the harm, but the impurities.

August le Loor is the man you go to in Amsterdam to get your goods tested, although there are 15 such places in Holland. These 15 centres share their information, so August knows what pills are around in what area, when a rave is being organised. He is also the man rave organisers telephone to get his harm-reduction seal of approval on their premises and set-up.

He arranges everything, from testing the pills to training first aiders, and warning the local hospital to have their ambulances standing by because there is rave going on. He never asks if the person wanting the pills tested is a dealer. He doesn't want to know. If he finds a pill which he considers dangerous, he telephones lots of contacts on the street to find out where the stuff is coming from.

He will then attempt to arrange a meeting with the manufacturer and, if the stuff still hits the street, he then puts a warning system into play, both at raves he attends and nationwide.

If you take a pill to August, he first of all identifies it by size, colour and logo. There are, for instance, 64 different doves. He can send the substance away, for spectroscopic analysis, and get an answer faxed back to him within 24 hours, or he does an on-the-spot acid test, which relies on the Marquee colour test. (We have since discovered some manufacturers are mixing chemicals in with the drugs to 'fool' the colour test.)

August is the first to admit that even the purest drugs are dangerous, and he uses his rapport with the clubbers to put across a prevention message. Every drug they present to him is covered by a fact sheet. He will never tell users a drug is good to use merely because it happens to be pure.

Our next call took us to a round-table meeting with Dr van Brussel and Gerard Schoulter. Dr van Brussel is the public health adviser to the Dutch government. On the whole, he seemed sad about the drug situation. He would, he said, ban all drugs if he had the chance, but that was impossible. He felt the only choice, after 18 years in this field trying to tackle the problem, was to opt for second best – that is, to provide what he termed 'protective public health measures'.

He was also very empathetic with us. He had a young daughter himself. He would, he said, prefer to cure addicts; but, as a doctor, although he knew what he wanted to do, he was unable to do it. He likened the denial of a drug problem in the UK with the grieving process. Until you reach the point of acceptance, he said, you cannot face the problem. He has a point.

I put it to him that every individual has the right to *all* the information, to make up their own minds. 'The problem,' he replied, 'is that when you are 18 you are physically grown up, but mentally still a child, so how can you integrate this wisdom?' Again, he has a point. On the other hand, at 18 you can vote, thereby contributing to national decisions; you can marry and have children. So when does the boy become a man?

Our next visit was to Jellieknet, the Dutch department of health help-centre. They have a lot of help available for addicts. They were putting into operation a year-long experiment to 'give' addicts their heroin and stop them committing crimes in order to finance their addiction. We never heard the outcome of this scheme.

Sunday, January 14, 1996: Dear Diary, Here we are in Amsterdam. Negative acceptance is wrong, i.e. 'Well, we've got the problem now, so let's show them how to take drugs safely. We won't go to the bother or expense of preventing it.' Positive acceptance must be a better way, i.e. 'Yes, the problem is there, and we must educate to prevent kids even trying it, but also, we MUST try and get people off it.'

The chicken and the egg. Amsterdam – which was first, the drugs or the problem? Did they have drugs and didn't handle it right, or did they deal with it wrongly, and therefore got drugs? We have a newly hatched chicken. We can't shove it back into the egg, but we can guide it to become a well-managed chicken, rather than an unruly cockerel.

We also went to talk in private with the mayor of Amsterdam, at his invitation. I think he wanted to get over to us that he personally was unhappy with the drug situation, and with the idea everyone has that it is all Holland's fault. His alderman, Mrs G. van der Giessen, who is responsible for many community affairs in Amsterdam, took us under her wing for the day. She owns part of a converted canal house, a most beautiful home, and her husband, who is an official city guide (and a Tom Baker lookalike, complete with scarf), took us on a walk around Amsterdam.

It is a beautiful city, but there are areas of it which look like something from Sodom and Gomorrah. However, if you do not want to see it, you do not go there. Most tourists, though, cannot resist the temptation of a quick look. To say the Dutch are open about sex is an understatement. I know you can get the same things in London's Soho, but I'm not sure I would want to see photographs of it plastered all over the walls, and girls plying their wares in shop windows.

One young lady, clad in cream coloured bra, pants and stockings, did her level best to entice Paul into her shop, with me standing beside him. A good tourist ploy, you may think, and she was quite happy to let me watch everything!

At night, the wrinklies disappear and the squares become noisy, colourful and vibrant, yet always with a very obvious police presence. The tradition in Holland, when someone is getting married the next day, is for everyone to put on fancy dress. One bloke came up to talk to the crew, dressed as a tomato. He was closely followed by a rather well endowed young lady in a boob tube, who walked up to George, busily filming, stood in front of the camera and said, 'Hey, do you want to film these?' pulling down her boob tube. George, totally uninterested, replied in his northern accent, 'Put 'em away love, you're ruining me shot.' It was an education to watch George. He would go to the top of the building in a freezing wind, or lie on the ground in Dam Square, whatever it took to get the shot he wanted.

The crew, and ourselves, travelled around in an enormous vehicle driven by a Dutch driver, who was good at polishing the knees of Dutch bikers as he passed them. At lunchtime one day, we parked at the side of Dam Square to observe the drug dealers. They vanish when a police car appears, then reappear like magic when they turn the corner. They openly deal, but do not seem to pester the average tourist, unless you make it obvious you want to buy.

Duncan, the assistant producer, donned his woolly hat, and pretended to be an interested buyer. He was secretly filmed all the time from the van, with sound as well. Duncan easily obtained the Ecstasy tablets, easy except for one tricky moment when the dealer led him behind a bush out of sight. He was even given a business card by another dealer offering him a better deal for buying in bulk!

This, in itself, was an eye-opener for us, but at night we drove around the back streets to see the really seedy, dirty deals being done for heroin and cocaine. This was your typical drug deal, warts and all. It was horrible. The addicts were such a mess and the dealers so callous. Take it from me, there is nothing recreational or glamorous at this level of drug addiction. It is a depressive imprisonment from which you cannot find a way out.

We flew home via Glasgow, to visit the National Drugs Helpline centre. It was very impressive, with many telephone lines, dealing not only with drug-related problems, but sexually-related problems as well. A call came in to one of the counsellors while we were there, from a young man with an enquiry about Ecstasy. The counsellor was very honest in his answer, but again, it upset me. 'If only I could tell the enquirer what he is doing to himself,' I thought – but he probably would not have listened to me anyway. At least with the helpline, when he gets in bother, he will ring back.

The last stop was to a really posh hotel, to take stock of all we had seen and discovered on our journey. In conversation, Paul and I were speculating again as to whether users would ever realise that having a good time was not about doing drugs. I argued that I thought they would probably say, 'Well, what do we do instead?' – and my answer would be 'What did you do before you took them?'

Ecstasy is not a panacea: it ultimately adds to their problems rather than solving them. They know, in the back of their minds, that sooner or later they must come off it. The alternative to that is to find something stronger that gives a bigger kick, and then they will be in for really big problems.

One thing that did strike us back then was that, although we now called ourselves a European Community, we did not communicate and did not look at each other's ideas, but we did spend a lot of time blaming each other. There is no time left for that. We must exchange ideas, look at what has worked and what has not, accept these evaluations and, instead of wasting time and resources on pinning blame on someone else, find out how to tackle the problem more successfully.

9

ADA is Born

Tuesday, January 16, 1996: Dear Diary, So fed up with MPs saying
we're losing the fight and putting down our country and our kids. We're
not going to lose this fight to a load of scum pushers. Give our kids some
credit for sensible decision making. Give our country some credit. Start
thinking POSITIVE.

Friday, January 26, 1996: Dear Diary, Went to Chelmsford nick to
receive £100 cheque for Leah's Appeal. Very moving. One policeman
found his son had tried cannabis and Ecstasy. His son intimated to him
that maybe he should chat to his other two kids – one in particular. She
hadn't yet taken it and he feels that's due to Leah and us. He was so
thankful, it made all this worthwhile.

We have gathered a wealth of knowledge and, as Paul says, we are like
software waiting to be plugged into a hard disk! We cannot waste all this
knowledge, but what can we do with it?

I have such a passion inside to help the kids drawn into this evil net and
the parents who are worried sick about their kids. But I'm not a trained
counsellor, neither have I money. I have no idea how to go about this, but
I know I must. I'm not pushy enough. All the media between them that
we have given ourselves to could finance the biggest centre ever, but they
probably won't.

I wish God would tell me how!

JANET: After a few more television appearances, we began to wise up. We received only expenses (for taxis and so on) when we appeared on television, and then only if we could produce a receipt. One day, however, after we were on a programme on GMTV, the presenter, Anthea Turner, was talking to us in a corridor outside a studio. Anthea had lost a sister, although not through drugs. She was very sympathetic to our plight.

As we stood talking, another producer came by and asked Paul if he would go to a club that night to meet some youngsters. He wanted to film Paul talking to them in the club. He offered to put Paul up in an hotel overnight. Anthea looked him straight in the eye and said: 'How much are you going to pay him, then?'

'What do you mean?' he replied.

'Well, he's just started Leah's Appeal,' said Anthea.

'Oh, of course,' replied the man, 'we'll give you a contribution.'

Paul offered to think about the man's request and he walked off. Anthea was adamant. 'Don't let them get away with it. If they want you on their programme, they can afford to pay for it.'

From then on, we followed Anthea's advice. More and more television and radio appearances followed over the coming months. The demand for our time seemed almost endless. Again and again we were being asked to make personal appearances at venues to talk about our experiences.

This prompted us to launch Action for Drug Awareness (ADA) as a vehicle to educate and help other parents and youngsters. One of the most important messages we have is that we are *not* there to tell anybody not to take drugs. Our message is: 'We will tell you the facts we have about drugs like Ecstasy. We will tell you about the pleasurable side and about the down side. Then you can go away and make up your own minds.'

We have to remember that the only reason people know who we are is because of what Leah did, otherwise no one would have heard of us. We try to show youngsters how easy it is to get conned into taking a substance. We describe how, in law, they are running a high risk of long imprisonment if they pass on drugs to others.

We speak about recreational drugs such as cannabis, amphetamines and Ecstasy. We talk about heroin as well, which many youngsters have been using to ease the come-down effects arising from taking the other substances. We are now finding some youngsters, who have become psychologically hooked on drugs like Ecstasy, are becoming physically hooked on heroin.

As far as the Ecstasy aspect of our talks is concerned, we have obtained videos which show the pleasurable side of taking the drug, youngsters explaining why they take it and how easy it is to obtain it. The tapes show what they look like, how they behave after they take it, how the drugs affect them and the music scene which usually accompanies the culture.

The talks are usually given in two halves. First of all, we give all the information we have already described, then we follow up in the second half with a message that people who take drugs are very selfish. We quote William: 'When people take drugs it only affects their bodies, but when they become ill or die, it affects everyone'. Then we tell them, 'This is how it has affected our family' and we show them the *Sorted* video. Afterwards, if time permits, we hold a question-and-answer session.

We have given so many of these talks now. At one stage, we were out five nights a week. We never go anywhere to give these talks unless we are invited. We have visited schools, colleges and universities across most of the country as well as a host of other venues. We have been to countless parents' evenings. The meetings don't always have the same format. Sometimes we might be sitting on a panel with, perhaps, a chairman, a doctor, a school liaison officer and others.

Usually, after a talk at a school, the teachers are aware of the emotional reaction to the *Sorted* video. In some cases there is not time for the questions from the youngsters afterwards because of the pressures of the daily timetable. In such cases, the teachers usually make themselves available in a later class to try to deal with any queries our talk of the film has raised.

If, at the end of one of our talks, a youngster comes up and says, 'Thanks, I didn't know about that', it makes it all worthwhile. Parents are often shocked. They begin to realise it could just as

easily happen to someone in their family as in someone else's. They
have been shown, in some cases, that their ignorance has deterred
their children from actually talking to them about their real or
potential drug problems.

It's surprising how many of the kids know, during the question-
and-answer sessions in schools, the answers to questions like
'Name the most common drugs. How much do they cost around
here?' Sometimes there are a few jack-the-lads. Paul might ask,
'How much would you have to pay for Ecstasy around here?' They
might reply: 'About £2.50 here, but I've paid a fiver in Manchester.'
You should see the faces of their teachers!

If we ask who has experimented with drugs, there is rarely a
hand raised. But if we rephrase the question to 'How many of you
know someone who has experimented with drugs?', almost always
some hands are raised.

*Friday, June 14, 1996. Dear Diary, After a talk in a school I was walk-
ing towards a young lad at the end of showing* Sorted. *He saw I was feeling bad. He was a 'typical' teenager – modern haircut, etc. 'Are you all
right?' he said. He cared.*

Some people seem to think the farther away from cities they live,
the less likely they are to be involved in drugs. In fact, the reverse
is often the case. This is *not* just an inner-city problem. Remember
what happened to William just outside his school gates? There is
less of a chance of finding a drug pusher among a large crowd of
people in a large city than in a small crowd of people in a small
village. In a village, the ratio of drug users is often much higher.
Moreover, in larger cities there are more drug agencies where users
can go for help.

We get a considerable amount of feedback from our talks in
schools. We are always open to constructive criticism of our talks,
that's the only way we know if we are getting our message across
sufficiently. Obviously it is important we have the correct knowledge to pass on at these meetings. For that reason we have spoken
to consultants and visited hospitals and laboratories. We have, for

instance, learnt much from Dr John Henry, from the poisons unit at Guy's Hospital, who attended Leah's inquest. Then, of course, there is a certain amount I was already aware of because of my own training. The Health Education Authority has also been a valuable source of information for us, as has the Drugs Helpline. Often, we receive information faxed from a variety of organisations if they think it might be useful to us.

The information collated from the *Sorted* questionnaire was from youngsters between the ages of 11 and 19, an across-the-board selection of teenagers. A lot of the information from the question-naires revealed youngsters anxious to know the truth about drugs – and they wanted it straight, not 'sanitised' as it so often is. Unless these youngsters get the whole truth about drugs and what they can do, they cannot make an informed choice, and that is dangerous.

As a result of the response to the questionnaire, British Telecom and Granada Television, who both played a major role in the production and financing of the video, held a big press conference to publicise the findings. Unfortunately, when they were asked by the press what they were going to do about the results, nothing was forthcoming.

We decided to ask British Telecom for a telephone helpline. A lot of organisations have such lines with trained counsellors at the other end to answer problems. We wanted to do something a bit different. We feel that, when a loved one dies, the last thing some people want is to be counselled, at least at first. Some people don't want their problems bounced back at them with comments like 'Do you think that's wise?' ... and 'Wouldn't it be better to do this or that?'

We feel there is a need for drug users to be able to ring someone who can listen to all the swearing and cursing they need to let out. Then, when they have finished, the counsellor might say, 'OK, I know exactly how you feel – I've been there myself. Now, where shall we go from here?' Not everyone is lucky enough to have family or friends nearby to talk to, so there is a need for helplines of all kinds. It's just that we feel that one like we have in mind would be particularly useful. We aim to build a databank of every organisation in the country that can help people with drug-related problems.

Many helplines may tell their callers, 'OK, I know now what you want, I suggest you telephone so and so' – who may be in an office hundreds of miles away. We believe it would be so much better to be able to say to the caller: 'We know exactly where you are coming from. There is an organisation in your own locality who can help you. We will call them and get them to call you right back'.

With ADA, we sometimes have days when the telephone hardly stops ringing, and then perhaps a couple of days with no calls at all. Often, the calls we receive can be quite time-consuming. People call us when they are worried or in trouble. We cannot say to them 'Sorry, we're just about to go out'. We have to be there for them. Sometimes we can be on the telephone for a couple of hours.

Paul and I are not professional counsellors – but that, in any case, is not what ADA is all about. We aim to lend a listening ear. If we can give them good advice we will, if not we try to put callers in touch with someone who can help them. We get all sorts of calls, the majority of which are from parents or concerned relatives. Some have been bereaved, the majority of them as a result of drugs, but we have even had parents who have lost their offspring from motor accidents or suicide.

I suppose they have heard us, in particular Paul, on television and feel we can help them. Many of them ask 'Why is this happening to me? I can't handle this situation'. They want to swear, cry, have a go about anyone or anything that has annoyed them. The point is, most of these people need to get something off their chests, and often it is easier to do so by speaking to someone outside the family, someone more detached. Many feel unable to talk even to their partners if their child has a drug problem. In our experience, it is often the fathers who try to shut things out, whereas the mothers need someone to talk to. That's where ADA often comes in.

When both partners know something is wrong but one feels unable to talk about it, it can cause friction. In the past Paul and I have had a similar situation ourselves. We had a blazing row in front of my friend Sheila. We were lucky, though – Sheila acted as mediator and helped sort things out between us. It wasn't just the death of Leah that was causing the problem, there were other considerations. It was just the way the tensions had built up and, sooner or later, they had to come out. If you are lucky, they do just that – if not not, and you are unlucky, it could split you up.

A drug death can literally tear a family apart. We have had calls from people telling us that their child has died but their partner and/or family is unwilling to talk to them because of the stigma often associated with a drug-related death. They desperately need to talk to someone before they go raving mad.

We have had many calls from people who have seen dealers operating. They may have reported it but no action had been forthcoming, so what should they do? I always refer such calls to Paul. Being a former police officer, he is better qualified to answer such questions.

Paul and I never ask each other about calls. We treat all calls with strict confidentiality. We only liaise when we really need to. If I don't feel qualified to answer a query I ask the caller to let me have their telephone number so Paul can call them back when he is available.

We frequently receive calls from parents who think their youngsters are doing drugs. We find the best way to deal with such calls is to ask why they think this is so. Gradually, as we talk, more and more comes out and, often a textbook scenario will appear – 'I think he's only done cannabis once, he's walked out of college' or 'He's got a different set of friends, he's not the boy he was . . .' But still we cannot say to the caller we think he is doing drugs. He could be, but there could be another reason – puberty, for instance.

Sometimes, of course, their children *are* dabbling with drugs. Often we hear the words 'We've just had a blazing row and he's walked out.' We respond by reassuring the callers that their children are not necessarily junkies. In their eyes, they are probably doing something like their parents do when they go down to the pub for a pint. Unfortunately, that is the way many youngsters see drug experimentation these days.

We suggest they get together with their children and say something along the lines of 'OK, we've had a row, now let's just forget all that and put it behind us. Let's talk about this. I've got a fair idea of what is going on here. I'm not stupid, and I need to know exactly what is going on.' We urge parents not to tell their children they must not do this or do that, but to make sure their children have access to all the information on drugs that they can possibly get their hands on, no matter how difficult it is to obtain. The children really *must* know exactly what they could be letting themselves in for.

We have such literature available to callers and we are gradually building up our databank of organisations throughout the country to which, if necessary, we can refer our callers. The overwhelming majority of youngsters will turn back to their parents at some stage, because they realise, in most cases, they will always be there for them.

Parents should always emphasise this fact to their children, because usually one of three things normally happens if they are doing drugs: they may get fed up with the drug and stop using it; they might grow out of the habit; or they might go on to something harder – and that's when they will need their parents more than ever.

Some youngsters have seen us on television or have been to one of our presentations and not had the nerve to meet us face to face in front of some of their friends – so they call ADA instead. Some say they have been silly and done something, others say they intend to carry on but can we give them more information? Perhaps they have experimented with Ecstasy or something similar. They may feel guilty and worried about what they have done. Some have been frightened by what they have experienced and realise they are never likely to do it again, but just want some reassurance. In such cases we don't really need to persuade them not to do it again, because they have already persuaded themselves.

It can be very distressing when we hear from someone who is in a terribly worried state and has no family or friends at all to turn to. We feel desperately sorry for some of our callers. That's why we like to think of ADA more as a friendship line than a counselling line.

There have been a few crank calls but, fortunately, not many. It is nice when we get follow-up calls, when people call back to let us know what has happened. We like to feel we can strike up a friendship with our callers and, of course, we wonder how they have got on after they have called us.

Sometimes people follow our advice but things have not gone quite as hoped. If they want to ring us back in such an event, fine, we'll always be happy to try to find another possible solution to their problem.

Sometimes we receive calls from newspaper reporters who are researching articles on drug related subjects. Do we know anybody who fits the bill for the angle they are pursuing? Quite often we do, but it is not ADA's function to give callers' names to the press. If we are satisfied the reporter is likely to produce a responsible and useful article, we might say we do know of someone, but we would *never* give out their name. We would always ring the caller in question first. If they want to help the press, we leave it to them to approach the reporter themselves. Fortunately, the press have always respected this approach.

We would like to establish a 24-hour telephone line. Unfortunately, our appeals for financial help to set up such a helpline have fallen on deaf ears. As Paul says, if we wanted to sail around the world or fly around it in a balloon, companies might be happy to sponsor millions of pounds, but when it comes to sponsoring something related to a drugs helpline, there then appears to be a stigma that many companies do not want to be associated with.

The ADA presentations do not always go entirely to plan. One such occasion was at Maldon, a local venue for us. Just before Leah had died, a young woman, Anna Woods, had died in Australia after taking Ecstasy. Her mother Angela tried to make the Australians aware of the dangers, but was having great problems. She contacted us after hearing about Leah and asked if she could visit us.

When she came over, with another of her daughters, she was accompanied by an Australian television crew from Channel 7. Channel 7 contacted us and asked if they could come to our meeting at Maldon. Mrs Woods came to our house and we had a chat and exchanged our news. Paul then went to the hall to set everything up ready for the meeting.

The producer, sound man and cameraman all turned up on time but the presenter did not arrive until the second half of the talk was in progress. He looked in a terrible state, almost like he had come straight out of a horror story, very gaunt and jet-lagged. He heard about Leah's experience.

During the question and answer part of our talk, the presenter asked if he could now interview us. Paul asked him to wait until we had finished the session. Perhaps that upset him because, afterwards, when Paul asked what he could do for him, the presenter launched a personal attack on us. 'Why didn't you tell about the pleasurable side of drug taking?' he demanded.

'It was at the beginning of the talk,' Paul replied.

'Prove to me all your facts,' demanded the producer. 'You said nothing about the pleasurable side,' he repeated. 'All you are doing is slagging it off. Prove to me you've got this research. Where is it?' He was very unpleasant.

We were later to find out that Channel 7 had given Mrs Woods the impression they had been filming us for a while, whereas we were given the impression they had been filming her at the same time and her journey over to Britain. In actual fact, they had not met any of us until that night. Paul was becoming very annoyed with the presenter and I wondered what he was going to do to him. Don was with us and was becoming quite worried. 'What is this all about?' he asked. 'Whatever is this bloke after?'

The producer, soundman and cameraman each came up to us separately to apologise for their colleague's behaviour. Channel 7 then asked if they could film another of our meetings as they would be unable to use anything recorded that night. Not surprisingly, Paul refused.

As we were driving into Maldon one day in August, the sight of some youngsters from a local school at a bus stop, jumping excitedly up and down at a bus stop, holding their A-level results, quite upset us. In fact, to be honest, it brought me to tears. That's when we realised, had Leah still been alive, she too, would have received her results that day. Suddenly, we had such an empty feeling.

We did actually receive a letter from Basildon College projecting her achievable results and, months before, in the November shortly after Leah's death, the Principal of the college, Mrs Woodrow, had sent us the results of her Summer 1995 AS Level examinations, together with a very nice letter. Leah had studied three science modules: Central Concepts in Biology, Transport/Practical Skills (Biology AS); and Organic Reactions/Practical Skills (Chemistry AS).

Mrs Woodrow and her colleagues had expressed their sympathies to us and wrote that Leah's spirit would live on and, by her gifts she had enabled other people to live an improved life. She also sent on the warmest wishes of the Students Union from Braintree College, who had written to her when Leah was in hospital, and hoped we would be proud to receive Leah's certificate on her behalf as it was a record of her achievements in subjects she had enjoyed studying.

Wednesday, August 14, 1996. Dear Diary, I sit here on our little boat at dusk. It's nearly dark and, above the crackle of the mud where the tide has gone out, I can hear raucous laughter and the rattling of bins and other property. I can see the flashes of lighters. A dark park is a congregating place. This is the reality.

I watched a perfectly respectable mum today, looking on while her sons picked up a yellow emergency telephone to see what they could hear.

Most parents probably believe their offspring are at their friend's house. This promenade used to be peaceful and safe. Now I find myself tele-phoning Paul to empty the boat hut every night. What is happening to us?

There are a lot of claims and counter-claims about the number of deaths caused by Ecstasy. We thought originally that death was a deterrent from taking drugs. We were wrong. It is not a deterrent at all. The ratio of deaths to the number of people using the drug is considered, by many regular users, to constitute an acceptable risk.

It is ironic that, immediately after Leah's death, the sale of Ecstasy virtually doubled, before reducing a few weeks later. The reason for the sudden rise, we are told, was because of the adrena-lin rush experienced by the users in response to Leah's tragic fate. When we tell youngsters that these drugs kill, they just don't see it.

For example, they go to a rave, they see how many go in and how many go out. It will *probably* be just the same for them. Nobody dies, so no problem. But they don't necessarily see the after-effects.

There have been a large number of people who have suffered stroke-like symptoms after taking Ecstasy. When the brain swells within the confines of the skull, the pressure can build up enough to kill, as it did in Leah's case, or it can cause a haemorrhage or damage part of the brain. As a result, there are people in hospitals who have lost the use of limbs. Death is not the only danger of using these drugs. But who is telling these youngsters the full story? Many of them just see the good side of these substances and have no idea of the risks they are taking.

Once you start taking drugs it's not always easy to come off them. Remember Helen Cousins, the girl who was in hospital around the same time as Leah? Helen eventually came out of it, was recovering very nicely and was getting over the embarrassment of being known as the 'E-girl'. She had a lot of harassment from the press but, within a few months of her discharge from hospital, she was involved in a car accident. The police found a tin of amphetamines in her car and the headlines started up again.

Helen strongly denied the drugs were anything to do with her but belonged to someone else, who denied Helen's allegations. However, early in 1997, we saw a report on the news that Helen had been to court and pleaded guilty to using amphetamines. Even her near brush with death failed to stop her from taking drugs. We even met a girl drug addict in Glasgow who had ended up in intensive care not once, but twice, and still had not come off the stuff. Early in 1997, we heard of a new marketing ploy used by the dealers. Extra-strength Ecstasy tablets were being sold as 'Leahs'.

PAUL: I feel very sorry for people who can stoop so low as to sell Ecstasy tablets as 'Leahs'. They must be really sick. However, I'm quite encouraged in some ways. We know when Leah died the sale of Ecstasy doubled. It was a kind of Russian roulette, a 'will I live or will I die?' syndrome. Then the sales levelled off and, a while later, they started to drop. Could it be our message was starting to get through?

I personally believe drug dealers were beginning to get a little bit worried. If their sales were dropping off, they needed a new marketing ploy. That's why I think the name 'Leahs' came about.

The first I knew of the name was in 1997 when one of the tabloid newspapers contacted me. My reaction? I laughed. Nothing anyone can say or do will upset me now. Nothing shocks me any more. The sale of drugs is a multi-million pound business. The problem is, lives get in the way.

I think Leah was a catalyst. When she died, the whole drug culture became a time bomb. It was something everyone wanted to talk about but not many had the bottle to raise. Leah's death was everybody's nightmare.

Because I am a loudmouth who believes in speaking straight I allowed (as did Jan) the debate to take place. Not everyone could empathise, but many imagined it could just as easily have been their child. I think Leah started the ball rolling.

JANET: But, it seems, no matter how hard we try to educate youngsters about the dangers of recreational drugs, there are always some people who, either through ignorance or the desire for publicity, make our job that much harder. I refer, of course, to the likes of certain pop-stars who have seen fit to publicly proclaim the use of such drugs.

First of all it was Sting, the former lead singer of the pop-group Police. He declared that cannabis should be made legal. The press went crazy. We were making our way to Ireland at the time and reporters chased us all the way to the airport to get our response.

The difference between Sting, however, and some of the other pop-stars who have come out with similar comments is that he was once a teacher himself, so must be credited with a certain amount of intelligence. We could not agree with his views, although he was also advocating drug education and awareness. He had obviously thought out what he had said, but, when asked if he would allow his own kids to use drugs, he said, 'No way, it's too dangerous', which we thought hypocritical.

Later, in January 1997, Brian Harvey, a member of East 17, one of the country's leading pop groups at the time, made a statement in a radio interview claiming: 'Ecstasy made him a better person' and that he had often taken up to 12 tablets a night. It was, he said, far better than alcohol because he could drive home afterwards.

Our reaction was one of pure disbelief. Looking back at our own kids when they were younger, they idolised their pop heroes. They wanted to dress and think like them. Then along came this lunatic saying it's safe to take 12 a night.

Soon afterwards, Paul was taking part in a radio phone-in when two girls rang in to say 'if Brian Harvey can take 12 tablets, what's wrong with me taking one?' What's wrong is that that's all it took to kill Leah. We believe people like Sting and Brian Harvey have a moral responsibility to think before they speak. If they take drugs and are prepared to face the risks they are taking, that's their business, but they should never recommend drug use to others.

Harvey's remarks led to radio stations across the country refusing to play East 17's records and he was sacked from the band. The following day an apology from Brian Harvey was released via his record company, which looked suspiciously like a damage-limitation exercise rather than genuine contrition. This suspicion seemed justified when Harvey was reinstated to the band a few months later.

If Harvey's comments were not bad enough, worse was to follow. Noel Gallagher, a member of Leah's favourite band Oasis, leapt to Harvey's defence, claiming that to take drugs was 'as normal as having a cup of tea.' He added: 'We've got to realise everybody is doing it, and when we do, it will be better for everyone.'

What a dangerous statement. No doubt some youngsters would have heard him and thought: 'If everyone is doing it, I'm missing out!' Oasis had given us permission to play their song 'Wonderwall' at Leah's funeral, which we appreciated, but Gallagher's comments made us feel badly let down, although we agreed with one part of his statement, that the drug issue must be openly debated. Like Harvey, Gallagher also apologised. We accepted their apologies – there was no point in not doing so. But, by now, the damage had been done. If only people would think before they opened their mouths!

10

A Hectic Schedule

JANET: So much has happened to us since we formed ADA. We have met so many people and travelled to so many places. We have met rich and famous people we would never have dreamed of meeting prior to Leah's death, right down to the most wretched addicts at the bottom of the social pile in the course of our efforts to heighten awareness of the drug culture. To detail everything and everyone would simply be too much for readers to take in. Let's just say our feet have hardly touched the ground!

However, some things just cannot be overlooked, for a variety of reasons. It would be nice to be able to put everything in chronological order but, because of the way things have worked out, this could often prove confusing. Nevertheless, what follows is, in the main, in order of consequence.

Shortly after Leah's death three men were found shot dead in a Range Rover in the village of Rettendon, which is not far from our home. The police quickly came up with the theory that the murders could be drug-related, possibly a gangland contract. You can imagine my horror when, the following day, the police arrived at our home in the course of their enquiries.

Needless to say, it was not a very pleasant experience, although they assured us from the outset they were sure we were not concerned with the murders in any way. However, because we lived so near to the murder scene, they needed to make sure they had covered every angle, especially as we now had such a high public profile. The press would be sure to link Leah's death to drugs-related killings.

Initially, Paul found the arrival of the police quite amusing. 'This is just my luck,' he said. 'I can just imagine Leah up in heaven giggling her head off at this!' But then he realised just how serious the situation was. Paul and I were both interviewed as though we were suspects. We were separated. Paul was taken into the dining room with one officer and I remained in the lounge with another officer. We had to go through all our movements on the night of the shootings in detail. On the day in question we had been to visit Leah's grave and had taken the pretty route back, which was unfortunate, as we had travelled rather close to where the incident had taken place!

When we arrived home from Leah's grave, we were interviewed by Tim Evans and filmed by a cameraman called Mike Goodman, both from Anglia Television. At the actual time of the shooting, Tim and Mike were at home with us, in our living room. We had, in fact, passed by the murder scene earlier than the shootings had been estimated to have taken place.

Later, on the day of the shootings, Paul had taken Emily over to Wendy's. There was snow on the ground and Paul was keen to try out the four wheel drive qualities of his Lada car, so he travelled the long way home, through all the country roads. He had travelled in the area concerned twice that day, and that was what gave us a few problems as it was considered he had taken longer to get back from Wendy's than he should have done.

We were asked to produce the clothes and shoes we had been wearing on the day of the shootings. Paul and I own two shotguns as we are keen clay-pigeon shooters. Our clothes and our guns were taken away for examination, as well as some live ammunition and our gun licences. I was even finger-printed. It was a strange feeling. I can understand how easy it is to become upset under these circumstances. I knew we were innocent, but at least, I understood why the police were questioning us – after all, I had been married to two police officers.

While I was being interviewed, the police officer asked me if anyone could verify my story. As we spoke, the news came on our television. Tim Evans appeared on the screen, reading a news report. 'There you are,' I said, 'he can vouch for me. He was with me at the time, and so was his cameraman.' We've seen Tim since and he told us the police did indeed check out my account of our whereabouts with him.

Worse was to follow. A short time later, Paul was told by the police that threats had been made on his life. I was not told until a couple of days later when a policeman turned up at the door with a little box with aerials and things on top. It had a panic button. The policeman spent quite a while fitting the box up in the house. The idea was, in the event of an emergency, we only needed to press the button and, in theory, the cavalry would arrive.

This was something I had not counted upon, something I had never even thought could happen to us. I could not understand why anyone would want to harm Paul. What had he ever done to hurt anybody? I just couldn't figure it out and I didn't like the situation at all. I became paranoid about this little button. I took it whenever we went out, just in case, when we arrived back home, something might appear suspicious. Like that, it was near and handy.

Apparently, there was a list of people in the drugs scene who had been causing trouble and it had been suggested that Paul might have leaked the list to the police, who told him there was a contract out on him.

I was especially scared for William. I wouldn't even let him walk down our lane on his own. I declare here and now that nobody can hurt me any more than I had been when Leah died, and I don't fear my own death at all. But, as for my kids and Paul, well that's another matter.

Paul made light of the threats. 'Oh, I've heard it all before during my police career, it just doesn't mean anything to me,' he would say. But, he added: 'If I was to come face to face with it, well, that would be different.' Paul handled the situation better than I did. I was just an ordinary housewife who found it all quite terrifying. Like Paul, I was still in a state of shock from Leah's death. So much had happened to us in such a short space of time. It was almost too much for me to be able to take in. I felt like I was on another planet.

You may recall my diary entry when the courier from a national daily newspaper arrived unexpectedly at one o'clock on the morning of December 28, because they wanted to know about the organ donations. It was so frightening, especially in the wake of the threats Paul had received. I had stood with the panic button in my hand and Paul was holding his shotgun as he answered the door.

There have been other unpleasant moments. We received a letter from a black-magic witch, who claimed she had put a curse on our family. When we showed it to the detective he said: 'Oh, I know her, she regularly curses me!' Thousands of the letters we have received have been very supportive but, of course, there will always be a few weirdos. One letter we received was made up of letters stuck on to a sheet of paper with a rather unpleasant message upon it. We passed it on to the police.

There have been many times since Leah died that our spirits have needed a boost. They were certainly boosted in February 1996. Our local newspaper, the *Maldon & Burnham Standard*, had a poll of its readers for nominations for the Man and Woman of the Year. Paul and I received the highest number of nominations, and we received the award at a presentation ceremony held at Colchester Castle. The award was the kind of thing we had never looked out for, or had expected to get, but the fact that so many people felt we deserved the honours really bucked us up. It made us feel people had taken notice of what we had been trying to do.

The *Maldon & Burnham Standard* is part of a larger group, Essex County Newspapers. The winners of the awards from the other titles in the group, and ourselves, met up at the castle for the ceremony, along with the Mayor of Colchester, and TV personality Esther Rantzen was there to present the awards. We took William along with us. We were given a nice lunch and then we were shown around the castle. Esther even took William down below to look at the dungeons. She was really nice to him.

The ceremony itself was very moving because the people who had been nominated by readers of the other newspapers had all done some quite incredible things. There was even a four-year-old little boy who had managed to dial 999 when his mother slipped into a diabetic coma. One man was posthumously collecting his wife's award. She had done some amazing things to raise funds for a local hospice. We looked upon it as a great honour that readers thought us worthy to receive such recognition.

I cannot remember exactly when it was that I sorted out Leah's bedroom, but it was a difficult task to perform as you might imagine. It was a room used not only by Leah but by all the girls whenever they came to stay with us or when we had overnight guests. At first neither of us could bear to clear the room but, eventually, it needed to be tidied up and I reached the stage when I realised it was a job that just had to be done.

It wasn't a pleasant job at all. I felt awful and cried most of the time as I did it. I emptied the room and put everything on the landing. It wasn't so bad sorting out her clothes, which were donated to a clothes sale for the church, but it was heartbreaking dealing with things like her jewellery, her school books and other personal possessions. Each item I picked up seemed to have its own story attached to it.

It must be a very brave person who can just throw everything out or burn it. I stored all of Leah's items in cupboards, except her jewellery which was shared between the girls and her friend Sarah. We let them pick out what they each wanted to keep. Months later I uncovered one of Leah's school books. It was such a strange feeling to look through it and read her handwriting.

PAUL: Yet another family now knew what it was like to grieve for their child. Andreas Bouzis, a 21-year-old youth, had gone to a London nightclub, taken Ecstasy, and died. His mother Josephine was Spanish, his father Dasos was Greek. When we heard of Andreas' death, we sent a card to his parents to offer our support. Josephine telephoned me within a week of her son's death. 'Mr

Paul' is what she always called me from that day onwards. Josephine just needed someone to talk to, someone who could *really* understand what it was like to lose a loved one because of Ecstasy.

Poor Josephine. She had been suffering from stomach cancer and was in remission but, Andreas' death had caused her to have stomach pains and sickness. On February 18, there was a memorial service for Andreas at the Greek Orthodox church at Finchley, North London, and afterwards in a hall at the rear of the church. We were invited to come along. All his family and college friends were there.

After the service we went into the hall, where Josephine had arranged an anti-drug theme for the gathering of the youngsters present and had asked me to speak to them. Josephine had also asked a leader of the Greek community to speak, and a doctor, who was a friend of the family, actually put together a memorial lecture that lasted for an hour and a half. It was very moving.

Afterwards, we went back to the Bouzis' family home. They were a lovely couple, very close to each other. Andreas was their only child. As we walked into their lounge we saw a burning candle in the hearth next to a picture of him. It was a memorial candle, the type of candle the Greeks put on graves, in a glass sleeve so the wind cannot blow them out. 'That's lovely,' I said as I saw it. Josephine gave us about four of them to take home. We decided to keep in contact with them, if only by telephone. Sadly, over the following weeks, Josephine's stomach pains worsened and her cancer returned. Within six months, Dasos had lost not only his son but Josephine as well.

Later that February we received a visitor, Assistant Chief Constable Clarke of Essex Police. ACC Clarke had earlier given a presentation about the Essex County Drugs Action Team (DAT) launch scheduled for the following at Essex Police Headquarters in Chelmsford. Unfortunately, due to other commitments, we had been unable to attend, so ACC Clarke had come along to repeat the presentation for our benefit, in our lounge, so we knew what was intended regarding the format of the literature involved and the form the DATs would take.

Considering the attention we had been attracting from the media, ACC Clarke was concerned we might have a different view about the way DAT was planned and was keen that we were, in fact, on the same wavelength as each other. I think he thought if we didn't like what he was presenting to us, our criticisms could attract media attention that might be detrimental to the project.

We attended the launch at the police headquarters in Chelmsford. A big marquee had been erected on a grassy area and inside there were a number of drugs awareness workshops. We found it very interesting to hear other people's views on the drugs problems in our society.

Towards the end of the month, we flew from Stansted airport to Glasgow. We transferred to City Hall's Satinwood Suite for the City of Glasgow Licensing Board's initiative 'Clubs Against Drugs'. Glasgow Council were not into harm reduction or drug awareness – they were into abolition of drugs – zero tolerance. They had persuaded the Licensing Board and other organisations, including Scottish Alcohol, to support the initiative.

Apparently, there were considerable problems in the city, with many young people becoming the worse for drink. However, they were coping quite well with the situation because they had BEDA (British Entertainments and Discotheque Association) behind them. They had laid down certain policy statements and criteria and were keen to promote them throughout Scotland.

There were still some bones of contention, though. One of BEDA's policy proposals was that there should be 'chill-out' rooms in discotheques. Glasgow City Council were opposed to this. While we were in Scotland, this was the main subject raised in all the radio interviews we undertook.

In the end Jan said to one of the interviewers: 'What is the difference between what we called a rest room when I used to go to Ilford Palais, and what you call a chill-out room? You are talking about something that should be there anyway for health and safety reasons, not something that clubs should be able to advertise as a facility with psychodelic lights for drug users.'

We believe that many club owners know damn well that drug-taking goes on in their clubs and use the fact they have a chill-out room as an advertising gimmick. Some clubs have been known to turn off the water to make people buy bottled water, so other clubs have claimed they have free water in these rooms so people could take their drugs 'safely'. It is like saying 'Come to our club because we leave the water on, we have a chill-out area and a first aider.'

While we were in Glasgow I gave a short talk, together with the city councillors, the High Sheriff of Scotland, the chief police officer and the BEDA people. As this was the opening of 'Clubs Against Drugs', we had been asked along only because of our profile, so I kept my speech short. I told them how refreshing it was to see so many organisations working so closely together to overcome a common problem.

They had some positive ideas and had reached a point where they could openly discuss the problems in the city, and their guidelines would go a long way to make people more aware of those problems, thereby lessening them. It was also encouraging to see them involving schools to help promote their message. I wished them luck and urged them to keep the discussions going, with a willingness to adopt change if necessary.

February 29 saw us at a recording studio in Wembley. Ronnie Brock, a musician from Manchester, contacted us. He sent us the lyrics and a sample tape of a song he had written about Leah. He had persuaded a studio in Manchester to give him some free time to do the backing music and then persuaded Wembley studio to offer its services free to record the rest of the music and song. Ronnie didn't want any money for his work. He wanted any money raised to go into Leah's Appeal. He brought about 150 children from a local primary school to do their bit. The studio made a tape for us and the finished product, 'We Say No To Drugs', was a very nice song.

Afterwards Ronnie was interviewed on BBC Essex but, disappointingly, the record was not played on any other radio station. We weren't expecting the song to be a chart topper but it was not unlike some other charity records. I think its message would probably go down very well with primary school children. It's a shame the record didn't take off because it was a nice idea in the first place.

Perhaps if the Spice Girls had released it, it might have been a different matter. I suppose, in this case, it was a matter of 'it's not what you know, it's who you know'.

Since Leah's death we had found very little time to call our own, mainly because of our commitments either with the media or drug awareness evenings and so on. However, in March 1996, Jan, William and I were invited out to dinner by Leah's best friend, Sarah Cargill.

We had kept in touch with Sarah and she had telephoned us almost every week. Her days of experimenting with drugs were now well and truly over. Her bedside vigil over Leah obviously had some positive effect in that respect. Sarah had spent the rest of the night in a police station cell after Leah had been taken to hospital and had been given quite a rollicking. A few weeks later, she received a referred caution for possession of Ecstasy.

Sarah had cooked the meal herself and it was nice to get together. We used to call Sarah 'the Shadow' because she was inseparable from Leah. They were like twins, everything one did, the other would do. Sarah had felt very guilty over Leah's death and had visited her grave almost every day, taking letters she had written as well as other little bits and pieces. She would stand by the grave and have a little chat with Leah before coming home and returning the next day. Without doubt, Leah's death had affected her profoundly.

If Sarah had held Leah down and forced her to take the tablet, she would have had good reason to feel guilty, but she hadn't: Leah had suffered the consequences of her own actions, her own choice. Therefore, as far as Sarah was concerned, we felt there was nothing to forgive.

Initially, Sarah had been afraid of me, especially on the night of the party. By March, however, we had come to a good understanding with each other and, if we had harboured any feelings of resentment towards her, we would certainly not have gone over to her home for dinner. Like us, Sarah was missing Leah badly but, in her case, she was still trying to come to terms with her enormous feelings of guilt.

*

March 27, 1996. It's my 50th birthday. I had dreamed of spending my 50th on a beach in Barbados with Jan, William and Leah, eating a Bounty bar. I had hoped we would have been able to save up to buy some of those cheap late-booking tickets so we could all celebrate my birthday in style.

Leah's death threw all those plans out of the window. By this time we were in the spotlight. Not that I'm complaining about that, because that was our choice, but the pressure of so many people recognising us as we walked down the street, sometimes staring, whispering or pointing as we went by, was beginning to take its toll.

Come the day itself, I didn't want any presents, I didn't want to see, talk to or meet anybody, I just wanted to be left totally alone. I had given everything of myself since Leah's death, as had the rest of the family, and I just needed this one day to be alone with my thoughts. I don't think even my own family really thought I meant it, particularly Jan. The girls kept ringing up and saying, 'We *can* come over, can't we?' and Jan was having to tell them, 'Sorry, but no. Dad just wants to be left alone.'

I chose to spend the day tinkering around at the bottom of the garden away from everyone, doing anything I could to try and switch off from the world. Poor William kept saying, 'When are you going to open my present, Dad?', but I just couldn't. William had even chosen a birthday cake for me, but it didn't even get cut. I think, for the first time, I had realised the full extent of my grief and I just wanted to deal with it in my own way. This was my own private thing.

Perhaps I was being selfish. Before Leah's death I had been forced to give up my job in the police force and my mother had died. Everything had been getting on top of me. The dream of that holiday in Barbados was something I had really been looking forward to, something that would have brought some welcome happiness. That dream had been shattered and, I suppose, I was feeling sorry for myself.

Looking back, I think Jan eventually understood my behaviour that day, but she was a bit annoyed with me with regard to William. Jan had had similar feelings at Christmas and again on her birthday in February. Although she had made the effort just for William's sake. It's just that she did not know how to explain to an 11-year-old boy why his Dad didn't even want to open his birthday card or taste the cake he had picked out for him.

Over the following weeks, my faith was returning stronger and stronger. I decided I would like to be confirmed. Also, bearing in mind that Leah was baptised in the hospital, we didn't want to leave it so long before William was also baptised. Jan, on the other hand, had been baptised when she was 16 years old.

On May 5 we attended our local church for William's baptism. Don officiated. He suggested we didn't make a big thing of it – we could slot it into one of the family services. Peggy and Hugh Rees and Alan and Jill Rose were his godparents and Wendy, Emily and Jan's mother came along too. In a way, it was a bit upsetting as it reminded us of the time we stood around Leah's bedside in the hospital as Don baptised her, but, other than that, it was a lovely service. William was happy. He wanted to be baptised and, within a couple of weeks, he and I were to be confirmed together.

JANET: The demand for our time from the media has been relentless. Every time a drug-related issue comes up, they seem, automatically, to want to know our views on it. We have met, or spoken to, all sorts of reporters over the past few months. Most of them have been fine, but, as in all walks of life, there have been one or two exceptions.

We have met quite a lot of journalists who are self-confessed 'users'. Usually we can tell just by looking at them, by the nature of their questions, or the way they talk or behave. Paul often asks them straight out, 'Are you a user?' and often they are honest enough to admit it if they are. They sometimes try to tone it down a bit, but we find that journalists who are users often produce reports like 'I think what the Betts are doing is brilliant, but it didn't convince me . . .'; or, on the other hand, their articles can be quite patronising, which is worse than being critical as far as I am concerned. After a while, when we meet certain reporters, we know beforehand what to expect from them.

Nevertheless, there have also been a lot of good articles. The national newspaper that initially reported most accurately on Leah's death and what had happened to her was the *Daily Mirror*. One of the most patronising articles was written by a young lady from a Sunday newspaper, which I will not dignify by naming. We met her at Wickford station, half an hour from our home, before taking her to one of our presentations at a school in Rainham on one of the hottest days of that year.

Although it wasn't one of our best ever presentations – the kids could hardly keep awake because of the heat – she interviewed them afterwards and, at least, their answers showed our message had seemed to get through to them. On the way home, she was asking us all sorts of questions – she was digging. 'This is a new car you've got, isn't it? Must have cost a pretty penny.' Her questions made us feel a bit uncomfortable and Paul's suspicions were aroused.

Over lunch, Paul asked her outright, 'Are you a user?' She admitted she was. She had been taking Ecstasy and cannabis. Even the next day when I telephoned her to discuss something, I had the impression she was high as a kite! When her article came out, I thought it was extremely well written but oh, so patronising . . . She wrote, if my memory serves me correctly, something along the lines of 'When I said goodbye to them at the station I wanted to turn round and tell them they had changed my mind, but they hadn't . . .'

Direct criticism I can take. If someone really thinks one of our presentations was a load of crap, I don't mind them saying so. That is their view, but a patronising attitude drives me mad! As I said, there have been so many good articles but, when a bad one comes along, it sticks in my memory. It's like news. Good news isn't news, is it? It reminds me of one of my diary entries, written back in January 1995:

Sunday, January 8, 1995: *Dear Diary, Lifeline quote: 'Dog bites man' not news. 'Man bites dog' is. 'Drug-crazed man bites dog' even better.*

11

Hello, Mr Major!

JANET: In the spring of 1996 the Health Education Authority was in the process of producing a *Parents' Guide to Drugs and Solvents*, which was intended to highlight the problems associated with the drugs scene and the signs of drug abuse that parents should look out for. We had been sent drafts of the publication by the HEA for our comments. The HEA is a cross-party authority that works with the government of the day to deal with all matters pertaining to the health of British citizens and they were interested in our views of how the drugs-education message should be put across.

The launch was to be at a theatre on the South Bank of the Thames in London in May, and we were invited to attend. On the day of the launch we set off from Wickford station, heading towards London. However, our schedule took a knock when, in the middle of nowhere, our train ground to a halt. We sat and waited ... and waited! Eventually, the train began moving again and eventually we arrived, late, at Waterloo.

We ran down the platform to find a taxi. We had to join a queue and then, when we found one, were further frustrated by a series of road closures and diversions. Apparently a foreign dignitary was about to arrive at Waterloo, so security was tight and the roads had been cordoned off.

When we arrived at the theatre, two people from the HEA were waiting at the kerbside for us. 'Where on earth have you been?' they asked. By this time we were at least 20 minutes late. They pinned some badges on us and one of them said: 'Just hurry up and get in there, we've held everything back for you and the Prime Minister is waiting.' We had no idea that the launch would have been held up just for us.

Inside, various drug agencies had set out their stalls. We were rushed upstairs to join everyone else. 'It's no use,' I told them, 'I've got to go to the loo first, we've been stuck on a train for ages!' After I had paid a visit we were quickly escorted across a room to be greeted by Prime Minister John Major.

Someone took a picture of me with him. He was an extremely nice man, although not as tall as I had imagined him to be. The Home Secretary, Michael Howard, and a few other MPs were there too. We all took our places at the front of the room for the official launch of the *Parents' Guide* in front of all the press and media.

As Mr Major was speaking, something quite amusing happened. One of the journalists in attendance had a mobile telephone that, when it rang, played a tune – he had forgotten to turn it off. Mr Major was halfway through his speech, when suddenly the strains of 'Oranges and Lemons' interrupted him. The journalist was desperately fumbling around in his bag, searching for his telephone. He was so embarrassed and turned the brightest of reds! I felt so sorry for him. To give Mr Major his due, he paused long enough for the journalist to find his telephone and switch it off.

I am not about to divulge my political preferences within this book, but I must say that, irrespective of anyone's allegiance, if they had met Mr Major personally and spoken to him, the Tories might not have been so crushingly defeated in the General Election of May 1997. He told us how sorry he was initially when he had heard what had happened to Leah. He thanked us for speaking out about the drugs scene and bringing everything out into the open.

When the ceremony was over, we were talking to Tony Newton MP and Michael Howard. Mr Newton asked us if there was anything we were particularly concerned about. I told him one of my bones of contention was that there was no legislation to stop the availability of pro-drug literature in record shops and magazines. I like to think he took my comments on board.

The HEA people had worked very hard to get this initiative off the ground and the launch had gone very well. As a thank you for our support, two of them took Paul and me to a little Italian restaurant for lunch.

The *Parents' Guide* was issued free to anyone interested. It featured information on what drugs are and what they do, the danger signals of drug abuse, details about the Medicines Act and the Misuse of Drugs Act and information on what to do in an emergency. Various drugs were described in detail, with pictures for recognition and, at the back of the book, there was a section telling where to get help or advice.

Prior to our involvement, the HEA's and the Government's anti-drug slogan was 'Just Say No'. After our research, we found 'Just Say No' did not work. Youngsters have to know what is happening if they are to make an informed decision. We offered our point of view and the slogan was changed to 'Know the Score'. We liaised with the HEA on the subject of Ecstasy and went on from there.

When the *Parents' Guide* came out, there was criticism from some quarters because it describes the feelings users can experience when taking certain drugs. Their argument was, if you tell them that, they will go out and do it. We take the view it is no good denying that users can get a good feeling when they take some drugs, because they do. If they didn't, they wouldn't buy it in the first place, would they? We felt it was important to give a balanced view.

A couple of months later, in July, we met Mr Major again, this time at a garden party he had invited us to at 10 Downing Street. I think Mr Major held these events a couple of times a year as a way of thanking people who had done something during the year about things that have concerned the public. He had also invited a few TV and show business personalities.

When we arrived at Number 10, the security was incredible. Inside, the building is wonderful, very impressive. One of the first people we met was the comedian Ken Dodd. We were having a chat with him when Mr Major and his wife Norma appeared and we all lined up to meet him. Afterwards, we had some drinks and nibbles and mingled. We met some interesting people, Cilla Black, Dame Thora Hird, and a lovely couple who had lost their son in the Falklands. They had formed a Falklands Society to keep memories alive of those who were lost in the conflict and to find out more about what actually happened over there.

Mr Major's secretary took us on a tour of the house and the Cabinet Room. It was the outside corner of the Cabinet Room that had been hit by an IRA mortar, fired from a van in Whitehall, a while previously. We could still see where the mortar had scorched the garden wall and the scars on the building itself were still there. The Cabinet had been sitting in the room at the time of the attack, and how nobody was hurt or killed is a mystery to me. Since the attack, the building has been repaired in the original style but with strengthened windows that were so heavy, the foundations had to be strengthened. The sight of the damage made me realise just how vulnerable our politicians are.

A few days later we were in Coventry. Andrew Lowe MP had organised a massive 'Heirs to the Millennium' gathering, consisting of talks and workshops in Coventry cathedral. He asked us to come along to give a talk on the drugs issue. The purpose of the day was to highlight issues that would affect youngsters when we go into the Millennium. There were many speakers doing their bit throughout the day and many, many people turned up.

When I realised we would have to stand up in front of all those people in pulpits, with microphones each side of the building, I must admit, I found it quite daunting. Paul and I had put together a piece, a dialogue, across the floor of the cathedral.

We played the parts of two 15-year-olds and portrayed their conversation as they looked forward to the weekend and going out raving. That led into us playing the role of parents and giving their points of view. We then ran a workshop in the audio-visual theatre of the cathedral entitled 'Who's for Ecstasy?' and later we gave a talk entitled 'Informed Choice'.

Some of the people who came to our workshop were impressed

and, as a result, July saw us travelling to Hampshire. Ray Hulks, a police officer, had asked us to come to the police training head-quarters to talk to some school police liaison officers. One of the other speakers attending was a man called Bob Mills, who worked for the Health Promotion Department.

When we arrived, we discovered we had forgotten to bring our videos along with us. Fortunately, they already had a copy of *Sorted*. Bob was there to talk about other kinds of drugs, describing how he goes into schools to show children what drugs look like. For some reason, he seemed very worried about being on the same platform as us. I think he was wondering what sort of people we were.

Bob is a good-looking man. He has the kind of face that makes you happy, makes you smile. Because he is a big fan of the late comedian and magician Tommy Cooper, his presentations are done in Cooperesque style. Bob likes to make his talks entertaining as well as educational. His talk went down very well. Now it was our turn.

Because we had forgotten our videos, I had to make do with drawing everything on a board and pretending to do the rave danc-ing scene from one of our videos. It turned out to be quite a laugh and everyone seemed to enjoy it.

Afterwards, Ray Hulks and Bob took us down to a little pub and boatyard where the BBC series *Howard's Way* was made. It was decided that, between us, we made quite a good team and arranged that, whenever possible, we would link up again for more presenta-tions.

Three months later, we did just that, at a three-day drug-aware-ness programme in a shopping precinct at Portsmouth. The precinct was on two levels, with the drug agencies from the area setting up their stalls around the top level. There was a lot of press coverage of the event and people came from far and wide.

On our first evening there, we attended a sixth-form college for a parents' evening presentation with Bob. Unknown to Bob, some of his managers were in the audience to see how the presentation went. When Bob eventually realised they were there he became very nervous but, in the event, the whole evening went very well and his managers were more than impressed, which helped Bob's campaign no end. They even agreed, if Bob needed to travel anywhere in the country to do another presentation with us, they would give him the time off to do so.

The same evening, there were four college students who, for part of the course they were doing, had put together a sketch about a teenage girl who was going through the stroppy teenage stage of her life and was mixing with the wrong kind of friends – a scenario which eventually led her to taking Ecstasy and dying.

By pure coincidence, the girl playing the teenager who died was not unlike Leah to look at. She had the same colour hair, cut the same way, and she was an extremely good actress. When it came to the part where she died, apart from the screams which I believe no one could ever reproduce, the death scene was horrifyingly realistic. It really upset me because it was done so well.

The group had written the sketch themselves and produced a wonderful and very moving performance. It was just sad that not one of their tutors had taken the trouble to come along to watch them, but nevertheless they were thrilled to hear how impressed we were with their performance.

12

A Little Triumph

JANET: September 1996. Malcolm Grey-Smart telephoned. Malcolm helps to run a drug- and alcohol-free coffee bar in Stourbridge, near Birmingham. He belongs to a church and his Christian group had decided there was a need for a place for youngsters to congregate where they could have a chat and a cup of coffee. The group acquired a premises, The Ark, and opened initially for one night a week.

This is no ordinary coffee bar as it has a prayer room to one side. Their ultimate aim is to make Christians of anyone who turns up, but they don't push their faith down people's throats. The kids go in and, if they want to talk about religion, fine. If not, at least they are off the streets and have the opportunity to make new friends. However, some of the kids enjoy the fellowship offered in the prayer room.

Malcolm and his friend Alan Adams asked us to come to talk at The Ark one evening. They had also arranged for us to give a couple of talks at two nearby schools during the day before moving on to The Ark. After our first presentation to some fifth formers in the morning, there was an incredible reaction to the *Sorted* video. By now we were getting quite used to the stunned silence which normally follows the video, but this was something we had never experienced before. Girls were crying all over the place. I said to

Paul: 'I know some usually get a bit emotional, but this seems really over the top. What on earth is going on?'

Then we moved on to the second group of pupils and were about to commence our next presentation when a woman suddenly turned up at the school. If I remember rightly, she was a drug adviser for the health authority, and she passed a message telling us not to show *Sorted*.

I wondered why not, so I went outside to see the headmaster to ask him the reasons for this objection. The woman butted in: 'The children who see this film will need counselling afterwards. They get so emotional. Look at the state of the first lot you spoke to.' I tried to explain to the woman that, if the youngsters left our presentation laughing and joking, we had failed. The whole point of showing the video was to make them think about what they had seen.

The woman was unmoved. By now, Paul was halfway through his presentation. The youngsters were very disappointed not to see the video. They had heard from their friends who watched it in the morning and were anxious to see it for themselves. We told them we were sorry but, we would try to come back again in the new year. Perhaps we would be able to show it then.

It wasn't until it was all over that one of the teachers came up to us and asked if we really wanted to know why we had been told not to show *Sorted*. He explained that one of the children from the school had died from leukaemia only a couple of months earlier. Everyone, the youngsters and the teachers, had been very upset over the child's death. Seeing the video had brought out their grief, as well as feeling emotional about Leah. They had received no counselling at all over the death of their friend.

However, after each school presentation, we were inundated by questions from the children and a couple of teachers. One of the teachers said: 'I think you have done some good here today.' We were later to discover that *Sorted* had been used by a large number of Personal Social Education teachers to teach youngsters about bereavement as well as drugs.

That evening we conducted a presentation at The Ark to an

invited audience of teachers, social workers, police officers, indeed anyone in the community who was likely to mix with the youngsters. The drugs advisor turned up with some of her colleagues. This time she watched the video and seemed to be quite impressed.

The next day we went to another school. Before we had the chance to start our presentation, a lady came up to Paul. She explained she was a PSE teacher for this school. Within moments she was crying in Paul's arms. It seems she had arrived at the school at the beginning of the term to be informed that as she was to be the PSE teacher that term and her responsibility was to teach the youngsters about drugs. She claimed to know nothing about drugs, the responsibility was too much, she just couldn't face it and didn't know what to do. She was in a dreadful state.

Paul suggested she sat down to watch our presentation and see what she could get out of it. Afterwards, he told her he would give her some literature to read on the subject. We were appalled to think a teacher could be put in such a position without any proper training, especially on such an important subject as this.

That evening, we returned once more to The Ark. This was a normal open evening for the youngsters. The children who had been deprived of seeing the video in the school turned up. There was a real mixture of youngsters there. Some were really hard nuts there, drug users, delinquents and so on who were playing billiards nearby even though they knew we were about to give a presentation.

A Central Television crew were there to film the evening's proceedings as part of a week-long five-minutes-a-night programme on the drugs issue. Paul and I started our presentation. The rowdy youngsters by the billiard table were quite disruptive and Paul had to tell them to either be quiet or go outside. Fortunately, they quietened down and began to listen to what we had to say and to watch the video.

One of them was a little blond fellow, a real little hard nut, but he looked pale and thin, the sort of youngster most mums would want to take home and give a good meal and a warm bed for the night. He had red eyes and nose. He had, I thought, obviously been

The injured bird that moved Paul to tears. It recovered and flew away.

With Esther Rantzen at the Man and Woman of the Year award at Colchester Castle in February 1996. (*Essex County Newspapers*)

Filming for *World in Action*, Paul talking with the Assistant Chief
Constable of Manchester, Alan Castree.

With August de Loor in his laboratory, analysing an Ecstasy tablet.
(*Duncan Staff*)

Our meeting with the Lord Mayor of Amsterdam in 1996. (*George Turner*)

Drug dealers openly trading in Dam Square, Amsterdam. (*George Turner*)

'Raider', one of our charter boats and Andy, our unpaid PR man, waving.

Sarah and Janet at the top of the Empire State building.

Paul and William with the Bishop of Bradwell (patron of ADA) at their confirmation.

As Communicators of the Year 1996 runners-up, with Ian McShane.

Here we are at one of our drug awareness meetings at Highbury College with pupils from Southdown College – James Cornford, Sam Carter, Rachel Ives and Steve Roberts are pictured with Bob Mills (holding certificate) after performing their sketch about Ecstasy.

These children from Squirrels Heath Junior School watched 'Sorted' and then entered a poster competition which we judged.

At a drug awareness talk at a junior school near Cork, Ireland.

With William, we have joined the church choir in our home village of Latchingdon.

Over £10,000 was raised by contributions to Leah's appeal to purchase equipment for the Intensive Care Unit at Broomfield Hospital.

Braving the elements on a windy Sunday morning in May 1997. Don (left) dedicated a tree in the churchyard of our parish church to Leah's memory. (*Essex Chronicle*).

sniffing something. To me, he just looked like a poor little chap for his age.

As the presentation went on, he quietened down and, when *Sorted* was on he went very quiet. I could see him watching it and things were obviously going through his head. As I keep saying, the end of the video is always followed by a silence. But on this occasion this youngster, being the clever one, made a big thing of crunching a big bag of pork scratchings. The other youngsters around him were not amused and their reaction obviously embarrassed him greatly.

When everyone started to move about again, I decided to speak to the youngster. 'Can I have a pork scratching?' I asked. 'Yeah, OK,' he replied, as we just got talking. We ended up having quite a long chat. 'I can't normally talk to anyone like this,' he told me.

'Can I take that as a compliment?' I said.

'Yeah,' came the answer. He asked me if we would be coming back. I told him we hoped to return in the new year and asked if he had been to The Ark before. He told me he had been a couple of times and, he thought, he quite liked it. 'I might start coming every week'. Again he asked me if we were going to come back and I told him we would. 'Definitely?' he asked hopefully. Then, over a cup of coffee, he started to tell me what he had been doing on the street. You name it, he had done it.

Paul and I began to pack up our equipment and, when we had finished, I went up to the young man to say goodbye. Not wishing to embarrass him, I held out my hand but he put his arms around me and gave me a cuddle. I had to promise him faithfully we would return. I never would have believed such a thing could have happened with such a lad. Since then, according to Malcolm, he had indeed returned most weeks to The Ark. Although he has not been converted to the Christian way, Malcolm tells us he seems to have enjoyed going there.

I consider that young man to be one of my little triumphs. There are a lot of kids out there just like him who are considered to be bad. Some of them are, but so many of them are so love-starved. They are so desperate to be shown some love, or at least sympathetic understanding, but they are not getting any.

Other things in life, like money and prestige, seem to be more important to the people who should be loving them. It is not just the youngsters from tenement blocks without two halfpennies to rub together that are love-starved nowadays. They are crying out for love and I would like to give it to them, but there is just not enough of me to go around. The example of the young man at The Ark really had an impact on me. I know now that there is no one in this life that is not worth loving.

In October 1996 we had a call from a researcher asking us to appear on the Maury Povich Show in the United States. It's an Oprah Winfrey, Rikki Lake-style show. They wanted us to bring Sarah Cargill along with us too. The programme was to feature other parents who had lost children as a result of some form of peer pressure. They fixed everything up. We were to fly to New York one day, spend the next day in the city, and fly home the following day.

On October 8, we flew into JFK airport. We had never been to America before and did not know quite what to expect. The first thing that struck us about New York was the noise. It was incredible and, as we were to find out later, went on around the clock. The next day, a very talkative taxi driver took us to the television studios.

Anyone familiar with the American chat-shows we see on British television will be aware of the near-hysteria of the studio audiences. The Americans, it seems, go in for hysteria in a big way – no chat-show seems to be complete without it. Among the guests on the show with us was a mother whose son had died through drinking too much, another whose son had died from solvent abuse, and a chap in a wheelchair who had been egged-on into doing something stupid while riding a jet-ski and was now permanently disabled.

Off set, as we were waiting to go on, Paul and I were a bit choked up. They had been showing clips of our children, prior to introducing us all and it seemed strange to think that Leah was being seen by millions of American television viewers.

The guests were introduced individually and told of their experiences. Incredibly, it seemed, each and every one of them could turn on the tears, almost on demand. Well, that is not our style at all. Upsetting as our experiences had been, the performances of the other guests seemed so false to us. The producer actually said to us, just before we went on: 'Tell 'em about the *PAIN*, we wanna hear about the *PAIN* Leah went through, make sure you bring out the *PAIN!!!*' It left us thinking, 'What on earth is this all about?'

Unlike our appearances on similar British television shows, such as *Kilroy* or *The Time, The Place*, as we have done on occasions, we did not actually meet the presenter until we were live on television. Maury Povich is a bit of a prima donna, it seemed to me, breezing on to do the show, and then breezing off without so much as a word to anyone afterwards. There was no rapport with his guests at all. It made us feel very uncomfortable and I think we were probably a big disappointment to them, we just couldn't put on a dramatic enough act.

Talking to the researchers after the show was quite an eye-opener. In America, the recreational drug scene is almost non-existent, apart from cannabis. However, they knew all about the heroin scene. The official average age of heroin users in New York was 13 years and it was a massive problem. They also had a rather fluctuating solvent abuse problem with junior-age youngsters.

It seems, from what we were told, that the recreational drug problem exists mainly in Europe and Australia. We were very surprised to hear that, for once, Americans were not leading the way in something and the researchers were astounded by what we told them of our knowledge of the recreational drugs scene in Britain. They told us about the problems in New York with cannabis and the difficulties arising from the drug cartels cutting out the 'middle men' and bringing in drugs directly from South America to sell them on the streets of the city at very cheap prices. Like our kids buy Ecstasy, it seems their kids buy heroin.

We had arrived in New York at the tail end of a hurricane which hit Britain a few days later. The rain was lashing down and the clouds were low and brown. I was very nervous as our plane approached JFK. Our hotel room was on the 23rd floor and the wind up there was quite incredible. However, the following day the weather was lovely.

We decided to go to the top of the Empire State Building while we were in the city. The view was magnificent. It was such a clear day and, from our vantage point, we could see the Yankee Stadium, the Chrysler Building and the Statue of Liberty. I couldn't help wondering what the landscape looked like years before all these tall buildings sprang up.

Although the pre-conception we had of the Americans was their sunny nature ('Have a nice day' and all that) we were a bit disappointed to find many people we saw were quite the opposite, almost gloomy in their outlook. Surely not all Americans are like that, are they? Suddenly we heard a couple with northern accents. When we turned around to speak to them, they said: 'Thank God, another English couple!' We were so glad to see someone actually smiling!

As well as our American experience, we have received a considerable amount of attention from abroad. We have been interviewed by television and radio stations and the press from France, Holland, Germany, Italy, Norway and Australia. Add Scotland, Ireland and Wales to that list and you can get an idea of the scale of the interest shown in the recreational drugs issue.

Some awards come from the most unexpected quarters. We received a telephone call from Joanna Hills, the press and public relations officer of the Royal National Institute for the Deaf who, along with Carlton Television, were holding an awards ceremony in London towards the end of October. Joanna told us we had been short-listed as Communicators of the Year.

There were four awards altogether, she told us, the Louder Than Words award for things done by organisations to improve communications for people; the BBC See Hear Deaf Impact award for people who have overcome their deafness to help other people; and the Communicator of the Year award, for which we were short-listed. Other candidates for this award were Kate Blewitt, who had produced a harrowing television programme, *The Dying Rooms* about Chinese girl babies who are put aside to die; Mr and Mrs Churchill and Mr and Mrs Hall who had raised public awareness of

Creutzfeld Jakob Disease; and Gwen Humble, the wife of TV actor Ian McShane, for her work to promote an awareness of breast cancer, from which she herself had suffered.

On October 22, we travelled to the Barbican in London for the televised ceremony with William, Don and Barbara. Television newsreader Alistair Stewart was the presenter and the judges were made up of the previous year's nominees. One of them was Fiona Castle, wife of the late Roy Castle. In the Communicators of the Year category, we finished as runners-up to Kate Blewitt. At the time we were being filmed by a BBC film crew for a *Matter of Fact* television programme. They were filming a week in our lives, so it was strange to have the BBC filming us while we were appearing on a Carlton Television programme.

Friday, November 1, 1996. Leah's 19th birthday – or it should have been. In the morning, Paul, William and I decided to go to Leah's grave. We met Don and Barbara there. William had taken a brass flower for Leah and we had taken some flowers and a card, wrapped in plastic. Obviously, some of Leah's friends had been there beforehand. Don gave a little prayer service by the graveside before he and Barbara left. As I have said before, leaving Leah's grave is always the hardest thing to do, and on this day it was no exception.

Because of the significance of the day, it had been a very difficult one to face. Apart from visiting Leah's grave in the morning, the rest of the day is almost a blank to me. However, in the evening, Ivan Sage, a reporter from our local newspaper, turned up to interview us for a feature about our lives without Leah, one year on. In a way, we were rather glad to have such a distraction, otherwise we would have spent the evening brooding as well.

Because Leah's birthday party had been held on November 11 the previous year, Ivan had assumed, as had many others, that the 11th was the date of her birthday. When he realised it was in fact Leah's birthday that very day, he offered to come back another time, but we told him we would rather carry on. Although we had often been interviewed for such features, we were glad someone from our local newspaper was interested enough to write an appropriate feature.

Paul and I had been intending to write a book about our life with Leah and our experiences since her death but our hectic schedule with ADA and such like just did not afford us the time to start work on it. When Ivan's feature was eventually printed, we felt he had captured our feelings of that particular day really well. He seemed to write as we felt. As a result, we suggested he might like to help us produce this book and, after some consideration, he agreed to give it a go.

13

Darkness and Light

JANET: Just after Leah died, I could not face going back to my job as a school nurse, so I went to see my doctor to get a certificate. I was still in an acute grieving stage and the slightest upset was enough to make me cry. The doctor prescribed some anti-depressants, but I never took them. I felt that, unless I got into a really bad state, I would make do without them and let my grieving take its course – let it all come out. Don't get me wrong, such tablets have their place, but I just didn't think I needed them.

I seemed to get over the worst of my feelings and eventually returned to work. At the time Paul and I were very busy. He was having to make up for lost time on his boat-chartering business, and I had plenty to do at work. On top of that, we were out six nights a week giving our ADA presentations.

However, just before the school summer holiday, things came to a stage when I became almost permanently tired. I was also becoming upset because William was having problems at school, caused by bullying. I was feeling really low. Like most other people at work, I thought I was just at a low ebb, as we all often are shortly before a holiday period. One day, two weeks before the start of the holiday, I was driving home from work after a bad day at work. I was fed up, missing Leah, and anything would have been enough to make me cry. The thought came into my mind that, if I were to crash and be killed, it wouldn't worry me – and that *did* worry me!

I don't know what made me think of it. What would happen if I were to drive into a concrete bridge? Who would miss me? Who would care? At least I'd be able to see my Dad. All these thoughts were racing through my head but, after a few minutes, they passed.

Over the next few days, I had a good few journeys when I felt just like driving on and on and saying 'to Hell with work'. But I couldn't do that. If I didn't turn up for work, I might get the sack. Then the thoughts returned. If I didn't turn up at work, who could care?

The holidays eventually arrived. Great, I thought, we can spend some time together on the boat business. Normally, being on a boat and seeing the river would have a calming influence on me; but now, although I was calmed by the river, it was also depressing me. There were a few days when I could not face the passengers on the boat at all and, on a couple of occasions, I gave Paul an excuse and didn't go. Other days I went but was thoroughly miserable.

The weather became very warm and, as a result, there were plenty of people turning up to go out on our boat. They were almost fighting for tickets. My job was to stay on shore to sort out our ticket system and wait to catch the ropes when Paul returned.

One day, while Paul and his passengers were on their way, I sat by the river and began to write. It seems that when I am distressed I produce my best writing, as my true feelings seem to pour out. It was an absolutely beautiful day, but I felt awful.

I knew something was badly wrong with me so, that night, I said to Paul, 'I need to talk to you'. And yet, although I knew what I wanted to tell him, I just could not get it out. It took me quite a while to bring myself to tell him how I actually felt but, by the time I had done so, I was feeling suicidal. I could not see any way out and just wanted to end it all.

I had never felt so low before, although when Alec and I divorced and my father died, things were bad. But at least, at the time, I could see the reason for the way I was feeling. Now however, I was in a black mist that frightened me, although I was not at all scared of dying. Paul seemed to think my job was getting me down and suggested I did not go back after the holidays. I did though and, on the first day back, I was feeling terrible. When I got there, Mary Peterson, our senior nurse, was already there. She had also had an upset during the holiday and was far from happy herself. We decided to go to the canteen to talk our problems out with each other, and there we stayed for the whole morning. After my chat with Mary, I found it easier to tell Paul how I had been feeling, but I had to pick my moment, just in case he was having a bad day himself.

Nevertheless, the black periods continued until, one morning, I got in such a state that Paul told me I had to talk to someone. 'If you won't talk to me, I'll ring Don, perhaps you'll talk to him,' he said, and that afternoon, Don arrived with Barbara. Don is a very good listener and, after a long chat, I began to feel slightly better.

There had been things festering in my mind that I could not bring myself to talk to Paul about. One was my experiences in the operating room at the time of Leah's donations. Another was an horrendous dream I had often experienced since Leah died that had seemed so real to me.

I was in a dark room with a table in the middle. William was a baby and someone – a dark shape – had tied him to the table and was about to take a knife to him. I was powerless, although I had not been tied up. I could scream but I could not move. The dream came to me more frequently and I would often wake up in a sweat. One night I was crying in my sleep. Paul woke me up and asked what was wrong, but I could not tell him, even though I wanted to.

Everything had been building up and I began to realise I was facing a serious health problem – a serious depression. I think maybe Don's talk helped me to at least start to see reality again.

By now, we had become friendly with Ivan and his wife Judy. I found talking to Judy to be very helpful in getting myself back on to this planet. She was a fresh face to talk to and we had a long chat. It was nice to be able to talk to someone who had been leading a relatively normal life, although she was about to return to work after a serious illness. After talking to her I began to see things more realistically. I still have days when I could have a good howl, but those suicidal feelings are now just a memory.

The experience has made me understand how people really feel when they suffer depressions and suicidal tendencies after taking drugs. Some people pooh-pooh the depths of such feelings – 'everyone gets depressed don't they?' I have often heard pro-drug lobbyists say such things but, until you have actually been through that kind of black hole, you can have no idea what depression really feels like. To bring that on yourself deliberately in order to achieve a few hours fun is worse, as far as I am concerned, than chopping your arm off.

Depression is like a prison. There are no windows or bars. You can scream but no one can hear you. You cannot get out. It is the most terrible feeling and it really upsets me that people can treat the subject so lightly. Just imagine being like that for ever if your anti-depressants are having no effect and no one can do anything about it. Dr John Henry, from Guy's Hospital poisons unit, is on record as saying that this is a scenario that concerns him greatly.

Paul and I have met a few parents of youngsters who have got into drugs and later committed suicide. They usually hang themselves. What a terrible way to die. One positive thing to come out of my experience is that, if someone rings us on ADA in a deep depression or with suicidal tendencies, I can honestly empathise with them. It's no good saying to such a person that they should 'pull themselves together' – it just cannot be done as simply as that.

November 16, one year since Leah 'officially' died, saw us attend our church for a communion service for Leah. Don felt it would be good for us. It would, he said, help us with our grieving process. He told us how relatives of other families in the past had found such a service to be very comforting. We could have as big or small a service as we wanted. We decided such a service would be nice. Paul, William and I, my mother, Peggy, Hugh, Sheila, Wendy and Norman, Emily, and her friends Jennifer and Emma all went along to the choir stalls in the front of the church. Unfortunately, because she was still in Sheffield, Cindy was unable to be with us, but otherwise everyone else was there.

It was a very cosy atmosphere, a very peaceful experience which gave us a feeling of closeness with Leah. Afterwards, rather than drifting off home, we picked up Norman's children and went for a pub meal with all the family, and Don and Barbara. We had a lovely time. There was no raucous laughter or anything like that, but we all enjoyed each other's company. How we wished Leah could have been there with us, too.

Every year, at the college Leah attended at Basildon, there is an awards ceremony to students who have achieved something of merit over the past year. In December 1996 we were contacted by the college to be informed that the Students' Union had decided to present a special award, in Leah's memory, to the student who had given the most, pastorally, to the college over the previous 12 months. We were invited to attend. It was quite a touching ceremony. The young lady who received the prize spoke well of Leah and how proud she was to receive the award. She told those present that Leah was a happy person and her death had affected her quite badly. She was a little older than Leah would have been had she still been alive. We were told that it was hoped to present the award every year and we offered to present it. We were so pleased to know Leah had been remembered in such a way.

Saturday, January 4, 1997: Dear Diary, The New Year dawns. Three new deaths. Robert Hutchins in Upminster, Nicola in Middlesbrough, and Birol Hussein Bhyat from Birmingham who was at a rave in Cardiff.

Accountability: BSE and E-coli cause fewer deaths than those quoted for Ecstasy, but the big difference is that someone is accountable – the Government, local authorities, health authorities, etc. With drugs, no one except the person taking it – but it's time people in education and health and crime-fighting took on board accountability.

80 per cent of crime is drugs-related. How much more does the Home Office need to pour resources into it? Project to 30 years time when our present drug-taking generation is trying to run families or hold down jobs as lawyers, surgeons, politicians, etc, and are taking up our health resources.

Moral debate – still no one makes the moral connection with drugs. Kids no longer seem to care about morality. You will never keep hold of morality while people cannot keep hold of their own minds because they are chemically altered. Is life all about pursuing one's own pleasures? Do we need a bill of rights? Moral code is not to make people miserable. As Rabbi Jakobinowitz said: 'People who feel they have something to contribute to society are happier'.

Politicians – stop wittering on about legislation that not many of us understand, and get down to the nitty-gritty of worries in our society. Take cars. You can manage on buses quite happily, until someone says to you 'You need to drive'. Once you have that car, you cannot manage without it, even though it costs you money, pollutes your environment, may kill you or someone else . . . still you cannot do without it!

Schools – You cannot have the same effect on kids if you are lecturing in something you have merely been taught or have read about. You need the real experts – other kids, users, ex-users, families like us. They have credibility.

Tuesday, January 7, 1997: Dear Diary, These three deaths have hit the headlines, because it is New Year and there's not much other news. What about the three in Kent, three or four months ago? The man in Southend a month ago? The near death in Romford a month ago? The people not put down as drug deaths, i.e. kidney failure, liver failure etc? What about casualty figures? Ask any clubber or DJ how many collapse in clubs, and get thrown out or taken home – far more than in any pub – on a regular basis, not just at New Year.

Birol Hussain Bhyat, an Asian lad, died at a rave in Cardiff. In February 1997, the city's evening newspaper contacted us to ask if we would come down to do a couple of presentations. When we arrived at the venue, there were masses of chairs set out but only about 70 people actually turned up.

Nevertheless, it was quite a successful evening, apart from the fact that there were a few youngsters there – led, I have to say, by an Outreach worker – who persisted in shouting down Paul by charging that he had not said anything about the good feelings some drugs can provide. An Outreach worker is someone from one of the drug agencies who goes out to clubs to advise about drug taking. This particular one was admitting to being a cannabis user himself.

We feel no one can truly advise if they are a user. Who knows what state their brains are in at any one time? They are bound to be biased towards taking drugs. It's like many smokers or alcoholics who are always looking for the excuse to believe it is harmless, so they can carry on.

As we have already said, our meetings are split. We always mention both sides of drug taking, the good feelings and the bad. Obviously these folk had not been listening. Paul replied that he was there to show each side of the argument. If they chose not to take any notice, that was their problem.

The Outreach worker went on and on, and the rest of the audience seemed to be getting fed up with him. Some of the youngsters with him came up to the front afterwards and were having a go at Paul. 'You haven't said how great cannabis makes you feel. It changes your life, everybody should have it!' Another said, 'Do you know what cannabis does to your lungs? It makes you cough and scours out your lungs. It cleans them out.'

At the time I was about ten feet away doing a radio interview. In the background, I could hear the nonsense they were coming out with and I was almost in hysterics, and so was the radio interviewer. We just could not believe anyone could be so gullible as to believe such nonsense. I could only assume they had been listening to their local cannabis dealer.

Then, one young lad came up to Paul. He had been smoking cannabis and taking Ecstasy. He told Paul he was trying to come off them, but admitted he was finding it difficult. He was overheard by one of the pro-drug lobby present, who called out: 'Yeh, but it's not addictive, you can come off it any time you want, can't you!' Paul said to the lad trying to give it up: 'Can you? I bet you any money you like, if I said to you now "You will not have it any more" – just like that – you couldn't do it. Name your price, I bet you can't do it.' The lad agreed. He couldn't do it. We felt so sorry for him because the other lot, his peer group, were influencing him.

The rest of the audience seemed to get quite a lot from our

presentation, judging by the feedback we received at the end of the meeting. Afterwards we met Karen Griffiths, who lost her son Byron after he got in with the heroin set. His best friend had died after using heroin and Byron was in such a depressed state over his friend's death that he hanged himself.

Karen, like us, was determined the matter should not be swept under the carpet and had started a local parents' group called TAFS to provide advice and family support. TAFS are four or five years ahead of our work with ADA and are affiliated to Parents Against Drug Abuse. They have now got to the stage where they are renting a shop from the local council where people can pop in for drug advice.

Karen arranged our second presentation, in Pontypridd, South Wales, which went quite well and was attended by several school governors. Karen's father owned the inn/club/hotel where we were staying that night and another one further down the valley.

They invited us to go to one of the clubs, The Black Prince, which, they claim, is as drug free as they can make it. Karen and some others search the female clubbers as they enter and the bouncers search the lads. The bouncers were very interested in what we were trying to do. The club was packed. God only knows how these youngsters stand the heat.

While we were there, the staff found a joint in the possession of one clubber and half a dozen temazepam in the pockets of some others by the end of the night. Those involved were told they either came in without their 'wares' or they would not be admitted.

However, the staff at The Black Prince stood no nonsense. Anyone misbehaving inside, were soon shown the door. Karen's sister had just arrived from a trip to Australia. She told us of the huge recreational drug problem there and, after stopping over in Bangkok on her return journey, was amazed to see the enormity of the problem there.

Good news! At last, in January 1997, Leah's Appeal passed its £10,200 target. It was a lovely feeling to be able to hand over the cheque to the hospital. I think we had probably raised a third of the money by taking up Anthea Turner's suggestion of asking television companies for donations when we appeared on their programmes. There were all sorts of other sources – fun days in the village; one man who sent in a cheque every month; the Metropolitan Police, who made Leah's Appeal their chosen charity one year; and a host of other people and organisations made donations.

The hospital decided to use the money to purchase a mobile ventilator for their new intensive care unit. They also bought a bed and a special heated mattress. The surplus money in Leah's Appeal was transferred to help finance our work with ADA.

14

The Irish Example

PAUL: Without a doubt, the most frequent demands for our talks have come from Ireland. The Irish have taken the drugs issue on board quite outstandingly. They have taken a pro-active, rather than a reactive approach to their drugs problems. Jan and I first travelled to Ireland a week before Leah's funeral, to appear on a programme called *Kelly Live* on the RTE channel, which is hosted by Gerry Kelly. We had been invited to answer questions about the drug culture in the aftermath of a couple of Ecstasy deaths in Belfast.

At this time we had not got into the talks routine. However, the idea was to interview us because we were parents and other parents wanted to know the signs and symptoms to look out for. We were asked how we felt, if we had any idea Leah had been using drugs, was there anything we could have done differently, how could Leah's death have been avoided, and many more questions of a similar nature. Also on the panel with us were a couple whose daughter had also died as a result of taking Ecstasy.

Following the programme, Jan and I returned to our hotel. Another couple who lived locally, Margaret and Bill, came up to us: 'We know who you are. If you would like someone to show you around Belfast in the morning, it would be a privilege if you would let us take you.' They were a very nice couple and, the next day, they took us around to see the sights of the city. This was at a time during the IRA ceasefire – the barriers had been taken down and we had a very interesting tour.

We returned to Ireland the following month. We had been telephoned by a man called Paul Foy, who is the area president of the Kilcock & district Vincent de Paul, which is, I suppose, rather similar to the Salvation Army or Rotary Club in England. Like the Salvation Army, members of Vincent de Paul are not afraid to put their faith into action for the benefit of others.

Paul invited us to go to Dublin to appear on a panel at a drug-awareness meeting in a hall in Kilcock, just south of Dublin, financed by the Vincent de Paul charity. The day before the meeting however, we appeared on another Irish television show, *Kenny Live*, this one hosted by Pat Kenny. On the same show as us was 'Madame Cyn', Cynthia Payne. She really is an amazing woman! After the show, she gave Jan one of her calling cards, which said on the back how sorry she was to hear about Leah. Another guest on the show was an author who needed the permanent protection of a bodyguard.

A radio presenter, Derek Davis, decided to arrange for the meeting in the hall at Kilcock to be televised as well. He was keen to highlight our visit to Ireland as much as possible. At the time of this particular visit, the Irish rugby team were to play against Scotland and our hotel was packed full of hairy-legged Scotsmen wearing kilts. I think the management knew what to expect because they had covered all the expensive carpeting for protection.

On the day of the drug awareness meeting, we arrived at the hall as some of the first people were arriving. Everything had already been set up and a big screen had been erected. It was as the meeting was about to commence that something unusual, even spooky, if you like, occurred. Jan and I took our places at the front and, gradually, the hall filled to the point that people had to stand in the aisles.

Derek, who was to act as chairman for the evening, was introduced. As he went to take his place on the stage, a butterfly flew upwards from the stage into the rafters. This was in the middle of winter! I know that in itself is not that remarkable but for me it had great symbolic significance.

I used to live with my parents at Ladywell, in Lewisham. Dad was working on the railways and times were hard. One of our pieces of furniture was an oval mirror. To brighten it up, Dad stuck half a dozen paper butterflies on the mirror, where they remained for years. When, years later, my mother came to live with us, the mirror came too, complete with butterflies. However, the day my mother died, all but one of the butterflies fell off the mirror.

Also on the panel that night were two sisters, Catherine and Carmel, whose brother Michael had died after taking Ecstasy, and Father Dennis Laverty, who assists a nun called Sister Concilio. Sister Concilio runs the Cuan Mhuire rehabilitation centre, in Athy, for drug addicts. Father Dennis brought along two of the addicts who were at different stages of treatment. Others on the panel were a member of the Garda (Irish police) and Gronya Kelly, who sits on EURAD (Europe Against Drugs). We showed our video of *Sorted* to an audience of nearly a thousand and it proved to be a very successful evening.

Paul Foy invited Jan and me to Ireland again in November 1996 to be interviewed on a panel in Kildare, almost a rerun of the meeting in Kilcock. A screen and loudspeakers had been put up in the hall in readiness for the evening's proceedings. Suddenly, the screen collapsed. As it did so, down came a butterfly which then flew up into the rafters, just like the other one had at Kilcock, and again it was in the dead of winter. We all looked at one another. 'She's here with us again!' I said. Paul Foy said to me: 'Once, I could believe, but twice is just spooky!'

Before we were due to return to England, Paul took us to visit a centre run by Sister Concilio. The centre is staffed by nuns and everyone in there has to go 'cold turkey' – in other words, there are no medicinal treatments, they just have to abstain from their habits. Basically, the patients have to stick it out.

One of the girls there – we'll call her 'Maureen' – was known to Paul Foy. Maureen was in a psychological mess. She had been at the centre for eight weeks, being admitted a week after her 20th birthday. Her first Ecstasy tablet had been given to her as a present on her 19th birthday. She had been taking up to nine Ecstasy tablets a night. Anybody claiming it is impossible to be addicted to Ecstasy should have seen here – they would soon change their minds.

Jan said she would never forget the way Maureen looked that day because she was about the same age as Leah, had the same hairstyle and was wearing similar clothes. Maureen was so pleased that we had come to see her. We had a long chat with her. She asked us if we would like to meet some of the other patients, and what was supposed to have been a fleeting visit turned out to last the rest of the day.

There were about eight other patients in varying conditions. Some of the stories they told us of what they had done to finance their habits was quite incredible. Quite openly, they told of some of the crimes they had committed, including robbery and mugging. Their stories had a big impact on us. One of them highlighted the link between rave music and Ecstasy: 'There is most definitely a link. When I hear rave music – even now – when I hear that beat, I crave the drug. Anyone who tells you Ecstasy is not addictive needs their head examined.'

The sister in charge had had tears in her eyes as she said 'hello', then 'goodbye' to us. She could not believe we were concerned enough to visit her charges.

JANET: In May 1996 we were contacted by Joe O'Callaghan, the Lord Mayor of Cork, in southern Ireland. He told us his administration had spent a year working with the health authority, the Garda and the education authorities to get a drug-awareness programme off the ground. They had produced a video, which some youngsters had helped to make, and an information pack was to be circulated to all the households in the Cork region. Joe wanted us to go out there to help launch their campaign.

We agreed to go and were met at Cork airport by the airport manager and Pat Duggan, the mayor's PR man, who had made most of the arrangements for our visit, a couple of councillors and city manager Jack Higgins. We were taken into the VIP lounge at the airport.

The press were there, taking pictures of us at every opportunity. As is usual in Ireland, there was an enormous spread of food laid out for everyone. The airport manager made us very welcome and told me that I really must use their loos as they were once used by the Queen of Sweden. Very posh! Everyone over there was so friendly. They treated us as if they had known us for years, and we soon fell in love with the city of Cork and its people.

We were taken to the Lord Mayor's chambers in the town hall and shown around. Then we attended another press conference, before going to the City Hall for the launch of the campaign in the evening. We were sitting with the mayor and mayoress, Jack Higgins, and representatives of the Garda, health authority and education authority.

So many people turned up for the launch that they spilled out of our hall into another one next door. The proceedings in the main hall had to be relayed to those in the other hall by television monitors.

Paul and I were asked to say a few words to those assembled. After our speech, we were afforded a standing ovation. Nothing like that had ever happened to me before, although Paul had experienced such an occasion once before at Rabbi Saffrin's event. I just stood there, not knowing where to look or what to do. When, eventually everyone stopped clapping and began to sit down, they presented us with a great big oil painting of a fishing boat by a local artist – they had obviously heard about our love of boats!

Paul got up to say 'Thank you', but he became choked up with emotion. Although I was rather emotional too, I could still talk, so I stepped in. As I stood there, I remembered a memorial to the war dead we had been shown in the Protestant cathedral that afternoon. 'This afternoon,' I said, 'we saw an epitaph in the cathedral that seems so appropriate to this particular moment with regards to keeping your children safe and with regards to Leah . . . '*In death there is victory*'. The effect of those few words was quite amazing. People were so emotional – everyone exuded such a caring, loving mood, and seemed able to empathise completely with anybody who had suffered a loss such as we had with Leah.

The following day there was to be an assembly. John Timoney, formerly the chief of New York police, came over to attend and we sat on a panel with him and someone from the Health Authority. It was a very interesting seminar, attended by a lot of people, including some who worked in the drugs field, and many parents.

John explained how he and his police officers had tackled the problem of four large drugs cartels in New York. It seemed the leaders were almost untouchable in law. But John was determined to do something about it. Eventually he and his men took out three of the four leaders by arresting them again and again for relatively minor offences, such as parking on a line, to bigger ones like tax evasion and money laundering, rather than going for the major issue of dealing with drugs, which would have taken so much time and manpower in order to build a case strong enough to nail them.

The drug dealers ended up with having their money and wares taken away from them. The police were prepared to do anything they could do to make life uncomfortable for the dealers. At least this way John was able to repeatedly remove them from the streets, albeit temporarily. Another method used by John's department was to make the offence of dealing drugs within a two mile radius of schools carry an automatic double sentence, with no right of appeal. This tactic was in response to calls from worried parents about dealers hanging around outside school gates. John claimed this method worked well and it was interesting to hear what he had to say.

Before we returned home, we were talking to a lovely man, Conn O'Leary, a councillor who definitely is one for the blarney! A shopowner, Conn is well known for being on the ball when it comes to council business and he is totally anti-drugs. He is a man who gets things done. He had taken part in the presentation of the oil painting to us. 'There's just one thing, Conn,' I had said to him. 'How are we going to get it on the 'plane, it's enormous!' 'Jesus!' he exclaimed. 'I hadn't thought of that!!'

A while after we arrived home, we received a telephone call from

Pat Duggan in Cork. He invited us to return as a thank-you for our help with the campaign. But we were so busy, there just wasn't time to do so until some time later, when Sue Harris – the producer of *Matter of Fact*, who had taken us to the BBC studios in Norwich the day Leah died – contacted us again. Sue wanted to do another piece on us, a year on from Leah's death. We told her about Ireland and, as a result, we returned there once more to do some filming with the BBC. It was so nice to see all our friends there again, so nice to go back.

Our visit to a girls' school in the Irish town of Trim, with Paul Foy again, coincided with the first anniversary of the 'official' date of Leah's death. We gave two talks and showed the girls the *Sorted* video. The girls, aged from 11 to 18, were very affected by it. When I had introduced the video I had mentioned to the girls that I would always remember where I was at this moment because, in a few hours' time, it would be exactly one year since Leah died.

When we had finished, we were presented with a book of remembrance. It was dark blue with a silver cross on the front, signed by everyone in the school – pupils, staff, the lot – and each of them had included a message. It was really lovely. All the girls had really taken on board what we had to say. They asked us loads of questions and told us of their experiences.

We visited two other schools to give talks in Kilkenny one day in February 1997. The first was a vocational school. It had been arranged that we speak to the whole school in one sitting. The talk was to be held in the gymnasium, a large room with a glass roof, and it was a very sunny day. There was no way we could use our screen to show *Sorted* because of the sunlight streaming in. As a result, the headmaster decided to utilise a television, which he had placed in one of the corners. Not a bad idea, except that 600 boys and girls were expected to watch it!

The youngsters were, shall we say, a bit lively to say the least and I thought we would have quite a job on our hands to keep their attention. Nevertheless, they all sat down and, when we showed *Sorted*, there was complete silence. The youngsters were good as gold. I'm sure they too, took on board our message, judging by some of the comments they made to us afterwards.

From there, we went to the second school, which was run by the Brothers of Mercy for upper-level pupils. There were, I guess, about 1,000 boys in a huge gymnasium-cum-theatre. It was extremely daunting to stand before so many people but, again, all the boys were good as gold and the end of our talk rounded off an extremely worthwhile day.

However, it was only afterwards, when the lady president of the Newbridge Conference of Vincent de Paul, Annette McCormack, said to us on our way back to the airport: 'Do you realise you have got your message across to 2,000 kids today?', that I fully appreciated just how worthwhile the day had been.

The Irish seem to be far more community-minded than the English. They are not frightened to confront the drugs issue head-on. They are determined to put the necessary financial resources into the battle against the drugs culture.

Nuns and priests in Ireland are, of course, still held in high esteem and they are ever-willing to take people with problems into their care as needed. Sister Concilio is a good example. She runs two drying-out clinics. Another nun, Sister Veronica Mangan, is setting up a similar clinic for recreational drug users. If someone with a drug problem needs somewhere to live, or treatment, members of Vincent de Paul, or the priests and nuns move heaven and earth to make things happen to help that person. They are not afraid to take over an empty building to use as a centre. They will beg or borrow the money necessary to finance their projects. They truly care for youngsters, unselfishly, Christianly.

In Ireland there are loan facilities for charities like Vincent de Paul which enable them to get projects up and running before ever having to worry about the red tape. Can you imagine the bureaucracy one would encounter in England if you wanted to set up a similar project?

And not only bureaucracy. We know of a case where a drug-treatment agency wanted to buy a house, it wished to use in helping recovering addicts. The whole village clubbed together to frustrate the agency and bought the house – which still stands empty.

The nuns and priests of Ireland deserve the highest praise for their work. They have provided an example of what can be done if the desire to do so is strong enough – an example we, in England, would do well to follow. Caring people like Paul Foy and Sister Veronica deserve all the backing that those who hold the purse-strings in Eire will give them. They put people before money.

15

Trials and Tribulations

JANET: The National Association of Registered Door Supervisors and Security Personnel (NARDS SP) is an organisation formed by Daniel Brewington and Lynwood Newman in an effort to establish a code of conduct for gentlemen usually referred to as 'bouncers' – the men employed by most nightclubs to eject troublemakers or to refuse the entry of unwanted clientele. Daniel and Lynwood, who are former door staff themselves, wanted to bring the bouncers' grading up to that of 'door supervisors'.

Bouncers have earned themselves a bad reputation which, in many cases, has proved to be richly deserved. It was not until we were working on the *World in Action* programme, soon after Leah's death and after watching a subsequent undercover *World in Action* documentary, that we realised that many bouncers are guilty of supplying drugs in nightclubs.

Barry Legg, Conservative MP for Milton Keynes, was proposing an amendment to the Public Entertainments Licences (Drugs Misuse) Bill, a part of which would ensure that bouncers, if they got into trouble, would be banned from working in such a position again. At that time, any bouncer caught dealing in drugs could be banned by his local authority, but there was nothing to stop him crossing the boundary into the next authority's area and finding alternative employment.

Daniel and Lynwood's initiative went hand in glove with the proposed bill which, if passed, would see this loop-hole closed. They wanted to improve the image of door supervisors by having them all trained to a national standard in dealing with first aid, courtesy, the law, how to apprehend people, and how to give evidence in the cases of people caught dealing in drugs. They were working on the theory that many young people are getting sick of having drugs thrust at them whenever they go out for the night. It was time to sort out the minority in order to make things better for the majority.

NARDS SP are keen to establish a good working relationship with the police and local authorities. They believe their initiative puts the onus on door supervisors to clean up their act. NARDS is hoping that if they are nationally registered, clubs will one day be obliged to employ registered door supervisors.

Daniel contacted us to tell us what he thought about the standards of door staff and asked if he could meet us. He arrived at our home with his wife and, before he knew it, Paul found himself roped on to the committee! When he later went along to a committee meeting, NARDS SP were pleased to think we were on board.

Later we received telephone calls from concerned door supervisors claiming there were drug problems in the nightclubs where they were working but that the management did not want to know. What should they do? As a result, Paul began taking on part of the role of NARDS SP. NARDS SP then had a meeting with the British Entertainments Discotheques Association (BEDA) who were not too happy about our involvement with NARDS SP. They wanted to know why NARDS SP wanted us if we were supporting Barry Legg's bill. They felt the bill could close down nightclubs. However, a letter from Paul to BEDA explaining the situation and clarifying what the bill was all about changed their attitude. In fact, in the end, I think they were quite pleased we were involved. Later on, in his absence, Paul was made vice-president of NARDS SP – how's that for a meteoric rise in standing!

Prior to the Christmas recess in parliament the name of each MP is put into a hat. The first names drawn have the opportunity to put forward bills, or changes to bills, they consider closest to their hearts or those of their constituents. The first names have the best chances of getting their bills through parliament. Barry Legg's name was the second name drawn and therefore stood a reasonable chance of progress.

The bill was aimed at closing a loop-hole and ensuring that if a club, or its door staff, misbehaved in respect of a drug-related matter, the police could submit a report to the local council in order to revoke the club's licence and have the place closed. Under the legislation at the time, if the club owners immediately appealed, the club could remain open until the appeal was heard.

One example was a club near London where drugs were openly traded by men on the premises wearing fluorescent jackets. The police put in a report but the club remained open for a further 12 months until the appeal was heard. Barry Legg's Bill was designed to bridge that gap, so that if a club or an area around it, or any person within it caused serious drug problems, the club could be closed down with immediate effect by the council and would remain shut until the appeal was heard. Only if the club won its appeal would it be allowed to reopen.

Basically, the bill was designed to give nightclub owners a kick in the bum, hopefully making them take more responsibility for what was going on in their premises and encourage them to get their acts together.

A nightclub was significant in the events leading up to Leah and Sarah purchasing the Ecstasy tablet that actually killed Leah. Raquel's, a Basildon nightclub, was the one in question in this event and, after a court case in December 1996, we became aware of the complex network of people allegedly involved in the tablets' chain of supply.

Two teenagers had been charged in connection with supplying Leah and Sarah with the tablets. One of them, 19-year-old Stephen Smith, admitted his involvement when he appeared at a magistrates' court in December 1995 and was eventually given two years' conditional discharge. Smith had told the hearing that a friend, 18-year-old Steven Packman, had obtained the tablets on his behalf from a dealer at Raquel's but Packman denied Smith's claims.

Packman's trial was to be held at Norwich Crown Court in December 1996. Paul and I received a subpoena to attend the second day of the trial. As we arrived at the court we were met by a barrage of cameramen. The defence counsel was unhappy about the media exposure the case was receiving; arguing that this was a high-profile case and that anyone involved might talk to the press.

As a result of his objections, the judge asked that the jury and all the pressmen leave the courtroom. The judge said that he did not expect anyone in this case would jeopardise it. He felt everyone would behave impeccably, the press included.

From that day on, although we were not required to attend the court, we felt they would rather we were there so everyone knew exactly where we were and who we were talking to. Not only that, we were anxious to hear the full story of how Leah had obtained the tablet that killed her. Throughout the course of the trial none of the press approached us, nor we them.

We were not after blood or revenge and we certainly were not after Packman, we just wanted to see the story through. Paul and I had heard the names of many people allegedly involved in the case – even some of Leah's friends whom we had never met – and the trial gave us the opportunity to put faces to those names.

We were not required to take the stand as the court accepted the statement we had made to the police soon after Leah's death. From our statement the court heard how Leah had named Stephen Smith as she lay dying. I could hardly look at Packman in court, not because I hated him or anything like that, I just glanced at him occasionally out of curiosity. I was almost embarrassed to look at him.

On the following day the jury, made up of six men and six women, heard how Sarah had asked her college friend Louise Yexley if she knew where they could buy some Ecstasy tablets. Louise asked her boyfriend, Stephen Smith, to help her find someone who could supply the tablets. Smith and Packman went to Raquel's nightclub on November 10, the day before Leah's party.

We were not allowed to speak to Sarah. We felt very sorry for her.

She had already paid a heavy price for what she had done, the biggest punishment anyone could have had. She and Leah had taken the tablets together, Leah died, Sarah lived. The guilt and hurt she feels is indescribable. Watching Sarah day after day in the hospital with Leah, talking to her and playing tapes to her, was heartbreaking to see. If any jury had seen what Sarah went through at that time, she would not even have got a caution.

Sarah spoke up well in court but looked nervous. She had to go through everything all over again and was forced to stand up in front of everyone, like some big criminal, to admit she and Leah had done it before. Although a lot of parents will not admit it, the girls had done what thousands of youngsters get up to every weekend, many of them taking far more tablets than Leah and Sarah, who were only experimenting.

Sarah got quite a grilling from the defence. She had already told us that they had experimented but, giving evidence, she surprised us when she told the court they had tried LSD. That did upset me because, used recreationally, LSD is nasty stuff. That was probably the silliest thing the pair of them ever did.

After nearly an hour, when she had finished giving her evidence, Sarah turned around to leave the witness box and her face just crumpled. By the time she walked out of the door, the tears were streaming down her face. Paul got up to follow her, but when he reached her she was being comforted by a court usher and he was not allowed to talk to her.

Giving evidence, Smith told the court that, once inside the nightclub, he told Packman he needed to obtain some Ecstasy tablets. A while later that evening, Packman allegedly bought the tablets from an unknown dealer and passed them on to Smith. The court heard from Sarah that she and Leah had previously purchased drugs both inside and outside the nightclub. The following day, it was alleged, Leah and Sarah each paid Smith £22.50 and he supplied them with a total of four tablets as Leah was on her way to her Saturday job at the Allders store in Basildon.

The judge had a very difficult job to keep the jury focused on what they were there to do. This was a complex case, involving many people but, at the end of the day, the only thing they were actually required to decide was whether Packman was the link in the supply of Leah's tablet between Stephen Smith and the person above Packman.

The main thrust of the defence seemed to be an attempt to undermine the reputation of the prosecution witnesses. One of them, Patrick O'Mahoney (known as Bernie King) was the head doorman at Raquel's. He actually stood up in court and said: 'Of course I've got criminal convictions – that's why I'm a bouncer'. Nevertheless, he was prepared to name names and he criticised the management and reputation of the nightclub.

The prosecution called up Colin Ball who was at the time the manager of Raquel's (which had been renamed Club Uropa after Leah's death). Ball had been a member of Raquel's' management team when Packman allegedly purchased the tablet.

Unfortunately, a lot of what King said was irrelevant to the question of whether Packman was the link in the chain. It made the jury's job much harder. On one side, Ball was claiming the nightclub was drug-free, whereas its former head doorman was standing in front of the court spilling the beans. None of this information had much to do with what the jury were there to decide.

The court heard how Packman, through the teenage grapevine, had heard King was after him because King believed Packman had told the police he had obtained the tablets from him. Via a network of acquaintances, Packman asked King if they could meet to talk things over.

I must say that, from what I heard of King's reputation as a very hard man, if I thought I had upset him, I would have been on the first plane to South America. There is no way I would want to arrange a meeting with him at night, or for that matter, at any time of day – especially alone.

The court heard how King agreed to meet Packman, but decided to take a tape recorder with him in case Packman said anything incriminating. He also contacted the *News of the World* newspaper to inform them of the meeting. King was asked if he would be prepared to be wired up so their conversation could be recorded. He agreed and it was further agreed there would be a press photographer and a sound man hiding in a car parked nearby.

Packman sounded very cool on the tape as he talked to King. It was a bit faint, but there was no panic in his voice. I couldn't help feeling they already knew each other, and the prosecution believed this to be the case as well.

The defence, however, insisted that Packman had been really brave and had faced King in order to sort things out. What was said on tape that night formed a large part of the prosecution's evidence. Packman was heard telling King he had not named him and that, if the police questioned him, he would say he was drunk and could not remember any of it.

On the tape, King was heard asking Packman a number of open-ended questions. He didn't say 'What did the bloke look like who you got the tablets from?' but 'Did this bloke have funny brown hair?' – a reference to a well-known drug dealer – who frequented Raquel's. Packman was heard replying that the man had brown hair.

According to King, at the top of the drug supply tree were Patrick Tate and Tony Tucker, two of the three men found gunned down in the vehicle at Rettendon soon after Leah's death. The other victim was their driver. It was about these murders that Paul and I had been questioned. Another name came out on the tape. It was alleged Tony Tucker supplied the door staff with drugs to be sold in Raquel's. Tate and Tucker were allegedly running the show with two others as their underlings. They, in turn, had their own runners.

After listening to the evidence in court, one thing became quite obvious to us. We heard how your dealer is, nine times out of ten, your best friend. In other words there is usually a chain of people who all think they are doing their friends a favour. None of them is a big-time dealer. They are just the small fry. Some of them are not even making money out of it, they are just helping their friends. But, in law, they are supplying. End of story.

It became apparent, the prosecution had alleged, that the link went from Leah to Sarah, to Louise, to Smith, to Packman (or whoever it was), before it ever got to the really big villains who wouldn't be so daft as to be caught actually handling the stuff personally. Maybe they didn't even know what they were doing was illegal, although I think they probably did. It's just not the sort of thing youngsters would do openly. Even Bernie King stood up in court and told the judge that these were not the people who should be in court, but the others he had named.

This is what is going on everywhere all over the country, week in, week out. The big dealers are happily making big money, and letting a long chain of underlings who run around getting rid of the stuff take the rap if they are caught. Everyone is so frightened of the big dealers and no-one is willing to speak up against them, so it is not very likely they will ever get caught themselves. Even if they are, they have the money to afford the best barristers available, so why should they worry?

The judge was having quite a job keeping the defence counsel in line, but I have to say the judge and both counsels were absolutely brilliant. It was quite an education to see them at work. I really admired the way they went about their business, and judges, from my point of view, really earn their money. I wouldn't want their jobs.

I felt desperately sorry for Packman's parents, Sue and Joe, who attended the court each day to support their son. In fact one day, I bumped into his mother by the mirrors in the court toilet. I wanted to talk to her but, the minute I saw the way she looked at me, I couldn't. I don't blame her because, from their point of view, we had put their son in court. We hadn't – this was a police matter. We had given no evidence at all against Packman, only Smith.

I could empathise with his parents all the way through, even though it was almost a 'them-and-us' situation. While a trial was in progress, defence and prosecution witnesses are not allowed to converse with each other. It was a strange situation whenever we went into the little canteen at the court. There were only about a dozen tables in it and the defence people, the prosecution people and the press were all in there, but nobody in any one group was allowed to talk to anyone from the others.

Sunday, December 15, 1996. Dear Diary, It's the end of the week of the Packman trial. Trial to continue. The judge is to sum up on Monday. My feelings for Packman are zero, except that, if he is the missing link, he must face his punishment like Smith, Sarah and Louise. What makes me mad are the fat cats at the top still running clubs and making money. This vengeful feeling is not Christian, I know, but, at the moment, whoever shot those three men in Rettendon, should be the one getting a medal. Whatever his reasons, he did the world a favour. These people are scum. When are we going to stop pussyfooting around with criminals' human rights and protocol and catch these people? Where has our British spirit gone? Are we just going to sit back and let these people run our country?

Perhaps our whole population needs a kick up the bum. Still the drug-using, money-making pro-drug writers write their snide little articles, telling all the kids how safe it is, what a good feeling it gives, and get away with it. We are ridiculed by them for being 'old-fashioned', for not wanting kids' minds permanently altered by these substances. People are dropping like flies with drug-related illnesses, suicides and deaths, but, Princess Di's new hair-do is more important to the media.

People who cover up casualties in their families should be ashamed of shrinking from the truth. We should all be lobbying to stamp on this. So, it upsets a few rich people and pop groups, the fashion industry, the magazine industry – TOUGH.

What's more important, a tantrum from the children when you take the sweets away, or letting the sweets choke them?

Dunblane, the machete attack, teacher Peter Lawrence's killing were all terrible. I wouldn't mind betting the perpetrators were on some sort of mind-altering substance, possibly even making money out of it. And so it continues, on and on.

Parliament is wrapped up in the election. It has tried to address the problem as much as it can without upsetting the voters. Which party has the bottle to really address it? To speak outright that it is wrong, and if big and famous people are found to be making money from it, to face this and deal harshly with them.

When are ALL our parties to tell us what they intend to do for the good of our whole population, not just the good of their party, whatever that may be? And when are we, as a nation, going to stop picking holes in anything a party tries, rather than back it up and give it a fair try?

There is no easy solution, but by God, for Leah's sake, and for all the other kids dying, injured, having their personalities changed, collapsing in clubs, committing crime and becoming different people, for all those kids trying to aspire to a peer-type depicted to them as 'cool', I'll not give up.

Nor will my family, friends, and everyone that knows us and can appreciate the true nature of these drugs – either because they have seen what it's done to us, or because they have seen similar results among their friends or family, from a death, permanent injury, mental illness, or the worry of a sick child, for whatever reason.

This trial has told the real-life story of a drug chain – not a soap drama, or a newspaper exclusive, but the truth of what is happening all over Europe, week in and week out. Leah's death was real. Sarah and Louise's cautions were real. Smith's guilt and sentence, real. Packman's trial and ordeal for him and his family, and possibly a sentence, real. A real life bouncer saying – quote of the year – 'Of course I've got criminal convictions – that's why I'm a bouncer', real. A corrupt club's management, real – and still our kids are taken in by it, that the 'buzz' is life's ultimate.

And still we mustn't upset them. Still we are being criticised for scaring parents. Still people are saying it's someone else's problem – we haven't got drugs in our area. Our kids won't do that! . . .

For God's sake, WAKE UP to this propaganda being fed to you by all parties who profit from it, either financially or by status, or both.

Let's tell people we are not putting up with this any more; we're not scared of you!

They didn't shove the pill in Leah's mouth, or spike her drink, but the underlying brainwashing of ordinary college kids like Leah, Sarah, Louise and the two Stephens, who just took pill-popping as the norm, that it was the thing to do for a special buzz on a special occasion, discloses a creeping rot underneath the way our kids have been taught and shown how to conduct their lives.

When are we going to stop pulling apart and analysing the individual corruption and tragedies in society, and look at its change as a whole? Drugs infiltrate into all walks of life. You don't have to be a genius to see how much worry and fright they are causing; how much twisting of ordinary people's minds; and before some smart-arse drug-taking journalist calls me narrow-minded, let him/her have a look at his own mind – has he really the same personality he had before taking drugs?

Believe me, I was narrow-minded 15 months ago. Now my mind is open WIDE!

The whole drugs business is disgusting. Why aren't we treating it as such? I would never turn away a kid who has done drugs and is worried or hooked – they need help. They have been drawn into the 'norm' of youth culture. But wake up, kids, the fat cats up the chain, the pro-drug people making money, however they are doing it, are disgusting.

YOU ARE BEING USED, NOT THE DRUGS.

At the start of the following week, the jury left the courtroom to consider their verdict. The judge had asked them for a unanimous verdict. From about 11am until 3pm they were out, but they came back to inform him that they could not agree. The judge sent them out again to obtain a majority verdict and still they could not reach a decision. The judge spoke to them about certain legal matters and asked them to come back the following day.

The jury went out again, but returned still unable to reach a decision and the judge had no option other than to dismiss the case. We were not surprised, quite frankly. By this time the jury looked like zombies. Everyone involved, from each side, was disappointed not to have everything done and dusted by Christmas. The pressmen were gobsmacked. As far as they were concerned this was like a damp squib. They couldn't even interview anyone because anything said could be considered sub judice.

The acting detective-inspector in charge of the case, Derek Nickol, and chief superintendent Brian Storey left the court together. Later that night they telephoned us to inform us that there was to be a retrial.

And so it was the matter dragged on until the following February. This time there was a different judge and jury. We decided not to attend this time around. We had already heard the story once and saw no need to go through it all again. There was also the fact that, if this was also to be a high-profile affair, it would be fairer for us not to turn up, or it might be thought we were after Packman's blood.

From what we have heard, there were slight differences from the first trial, one of which was there was now a written statement from the forensic laboratory that had tested samples taken from Leah that emphasised that her tablet was a normal strength of 113 milligrams and, was, according to prosecuting counsel Andrew Williams, 'pure and unadulterated Ecstasy'.

We were led to believe there would be a verdict on the Thursday, so we decided we would be there to hear it. However, things were going slower than had been expected and all we heard were both counsels summing up, although it was very interesting.

Because I had other plans, Paul decided he would return the following day for the verdict. I had already guessed something had been going on, because it was late in the day when Paul telephoned me to say there had been another hung jury. Because it was a retrial, the judge had to rule a verdict of not guilty.

I was not surprised and, in a strange sort of way, I was almost relieved for Packman. He and his family had been through so much. No parent would ever want to think their own child could be guilty of such a thing. I know if it had been William standing accused in the dock, I would have wanted to be there for him, no matter what he had done.

As a parent I have some idea of what Joe and Sue Packman were going through. They would never believe their son had ever done anything wrong. Nothing anyone could have done to Packman would have brought Leah back, so for Paul and me the verdict was almost an irrelevance. We were more disappointed that the big boys at the top of the drugs business were still at large and, seemingly, untouchable.

During the trial Packman had spoken of his sadness and distress over Leah's death, and afterwards his family's lawyer read out a statement for the press: 'The past 15 months have been a torment to Steven Packman and his parents. This is a decent young man and a decent family. They are now relieved that this is at an end and that Steven Packman leaves this court an innocent man. To them, drugs are a great evil in our society and they implore the police to detect and arrest the dealers'.

Acting DI Nickol told the press that if any new evidence was found regarding the source of the drugs which killed Leah, it would be acted upon. He told pressmen that the decision for the retrial was made by the Crown Prosecution Service. 'I do hope, at the end of the day, this will be a warning to people that dabbling in controlled substances has got its inherent dangers,' he added.

PAUL: The Misuse of Drugs Act 1971 gives police the powers to stop, search and retain. It defines what a legal drug is and puts drugs into classes A, B and C. The sentence on conviction of possession of a Class A drug with intent to supply, such as heroin, cocaine, Ecstasy and amphetamine (if it is for injection), is life imprisonment. Possession of any of the above for one's own use is seven years. The law doesn't need to be any stronger than that. Compare this, for instance, to the recent case where two early-teenage girls were sentenced to a derisory two years in prison for kicking another girl to death – and were released for good behaviour in 1997 after just 12 months. *The deterrent isn't the law, it's the interpretation of the law in terms of sentencing policy.*

Consider next the little-used Drug Trafficking Act of 1986. In simple terms this law states that any property, be it a house, a car or whatever, obtained through transactions of illegal drugs, can be seized by the police, and the courts then have the power to forfeit such goods to auction them off in order to put the proceeds to good use.

However, the authorities often appear reluctant to bring this law into play. Perhaps they feel it doesn't seem politically correct to do so. Consequently, I believe, the police are also loath to take it before the courts and ask for it.

We have here a marvellous act that, *if used*, could be of benefit to organisations such as the National Health Service, by confiscating millions of pounds from some big drugs baron. For a drug dealer to pay a £2,000 fine is nothing – it's just an hour's work. I feel the judiciary have to accept some of the blame for this situation. You could put an identical case before ten different courts and come up with ten different sentences. That is a human failing. That is what happens when magistrates put their own, sometimes wayward interpretation upon a piece of legislation.

Let us take an absurd hypothetical scenario. If you came up before a judge who was fond of snorting cocaine, he might interpret the Misuse of Drugs Act in a fairly lenient way because he was himself a drug user. At the other end of the scale, if you found yourself before a judge who had lost a relative through drug misuse, he might put you away for 20 years.

I believe a person should have three bites of the cherry and, if they step over the line for the fourth time they should automatically receive a prison sentence of a mandatory length. Then people would know exactly where they stand.

I would not say there should be just one immediate mandatory sentence. On a first offence, there might be mitigating circumstances which should be taken into account. But we should weigh up the offence with the sentence passed. For example, going back to those girls sentenced to two years for kicking the other girl to death. Nothing can persuade me that two years fits that crime.

Perhaps the courts are so concerned about the perpetrators' rights that the victims' rights are forgotten. I think it's about time the majority started to shout out to the people that matter that they are getting things back to front.

If I could wave a magic wand, I would make every person realise that life is the most precious and wondrous gift anybody could be given, whether they be rich or poor. There should never be a need for a mind-altering substance. A healthy life is even more precious.

Taking any drug is potentially damaging to that health and puts the user on to a false plane. Youngsters are being sold the myth that the life they have is not enough, and that a higher level of existence is obtainable simply by taking something from a packet, out of a bottle, or through a hollow needle. It's a lie. Simple, ordinary happiness and love doesn't seem to be enough any more and that is very sad. Health is one of those things many don't realise is precious until they lose it.

16

Sarah's Lesson in Life

JANET: It makes us wonder why youngsters these days are still prepared to risk their lives by taking drugs. Do they really want to end up like Maureen at Sister Concilio's centre or, worse still, like Leah? The issue of recreational drugs and the dangers associated with them has received considerable attention since Leah's death, but still, it seems, many are prepared to take the ultimate gamble. Perhaps Leah and Sarah should have been more aware of the dangers in what they were doing but, it has to be said, the level of awareness at that time was nothing like it is now. We could go on and on as to why youngsters take drugs but we are just old fogeys, aren't we? How do we really know what goes on in a teenager's head?

Although younger readers may not find our theories credible, perhaps they will take notice of someone more their own age. For that reason we have asked Sarah to explain why she and Leah experimented in the first place, how often they indulged in drug abuse, and what she now thinks of the consequences of their actions.

As you can imagine, the press hounded Sarah, particularly around the time of Leah's death and the funeral, and again at the trial of the men accused of supplying them with the Ecstasy tablets and subsequent retrial. In spite of her reluctance to talk to the press, she has agreed to speak out for the purposes of this book and we are truly grateful for that. This is her story.

SARAH: I first met Leah at school when we were in the third or fourth year. Her mother had just died. I would say Leah was just like any other normal teenager. Generally, she was very outgoing and liked to have a good time. She was very friendly and would do anything to help her friends. When we were together we would go out to various clubs or pubs, or sometimes we would just hang around with some of our friends.

The year before she died we went to Spain for a holiday. We stayed in Benidorm and had a wonderful time. We met loads of people there and went to several nightclubs. By the end of the week we had nearly worn ourselves out. We did all the sort of things most normal teenagers would do in Spain, staying up most of the night in discotheques and so on.

Although we were out so much, we never touched anything like drugs at all; in fact our first experiences of drugs did not come until after the holiday. We enjoyed it so much in Spain we decided to book up to return the following year but, unfortunately, the booking had to be cancelled because of Leah's death.

I can't remember what it was we experimented with first of all, although I think it was probably cannabis. Later we tried LSD and then one night, when LSD was not available, we bought a couple of Ecstasy tablets. That was the first time we had taken Ecstasy. I suppose we bought it on about five occasions in all. Leah and I always had exactly the same as far as drugs were concerned. We bought them together and shared them.

I'm sure Leah didn't take any form of drug because of me. She was at a different college to me at the time and had heard from her college friends about the effects of different substances. So had I, and so, out of curiosity, we both decided to experiment. I honestly do not remember who first suggested trying anything out. We were not nervous when we puffed the cannabis, but with Ecstasy, and the other drugs, we were. Nevertheless, it gave us a bit of a buzz to experiment.

I suppose cannabis and Ecstasy are, or were when we were doing them, the most popular drugs among teenagers; and there are many who go out at weekends to try them out or are already doing it. If they go into a nightclub it is more than likely they will be offered something. Rave music is very fast so you need to dance fast. That's why Ecstasy is so popular, it gives you so much energy. There is always a demand for it. I'm sure most of them take it first of all out of curiosity or because they don't want to be the odd one out.

On the night of Leah's party, we were getting ready in Leah's bedroom. About 7.45pm, while we were alone, we decided to take an Ecstasy tablet. This time, the tablets had an apple motif on them. We had both taken Ecstasy before but this was the first time we had had tablets with the apple motif. I had heard they were stronger than some of the others. By now, we had each had the experience of taking a complete tablet but, as we had never taken one with the apple motif before, I suggested to Leah we break one in half. 'Don't worry', she said, 'we've had a whole one before', so we each took a whole tablet.

Although William has said Leah would not keep still at the party, she did not dance a lot. She was talking with all her friends and was very chatty. I was also feeling the effects of the tablet, but not as much as I was expecting to. I thought it would be more noticeable if the apples were supposed to be stronger. I didn't mind though because I was having a good time, even though I wasn't dancing much.

Later in the evening, Leah asked me to come upstairs with her to get a drink of water but, as she got near to the top of the stairs, her legs gave way and she stumbled. I picked her up and helped her into the bathroom to get some water. She told me she couldn't feel her legs properly. Then she was sick down the toilet. She began to get worried and started to panic. She could barely talk but she managed to tell me her head was really hurting. She asked me to get her mum, but I didn't know whether to or not.

I was panicking, really scared. I could tell just by looking at her eyes that something was seriously wrong. I sent William downstairs to get Jan. When Paul came upstairs he met me in his bedroom and asked me what Leah had taken. I told him. Jan was in the bathroom with Leah who had already told her what she had taken, but she was murmuring and Paul needed to double-check. There was no point in lying. Paul wasn't panicking at the time. Perhaps he thought Leah would be OK and so did I. But when she wouldn't stop being sick and finally collapsed on the bathroom floor, she seemed to have a fit and I got really scared and ran downstairs.

In the lounge the others had realised something was wrong. Jan had called the ambulance and a couple of the lads went down the lane to meet it. By now, the effects of the Ecstasy I had taken had disappeared, probably because of the shock. I just couldn't stop crying. I was scared, feeling guilty. I kept thinking, if only I had taken Leah's tablet instead. Perhaps I could have coped with it better because, if it was a faulty tablet, I am a much bigger person than her. (As it turned out later, tests proved the tablet Leah had taken was pure Ecstasy.)

We were all sitting in the front room, very upset, when Paul came downstairs. I can't remember exactly what he said, but he was furious. I was so scared and I wouldn't have blamed him if he had gone for me. However, as Leah was taken away in the ambulance, I asked him if she was going to be all right. 'I hope so,' he said, and he gave me a cuddle.

As soon as the police arrived, I went up to them to tell them about the Ecstasy. I showed them the remaining two tablets – we had bought four altogether – because I knew they would probably need them to do tests or whatever. The police said something along the lines of 'You have the right to remain silent' and something about me being in possession of two Ecstasy tablets. I was taken to Southminster police station. There they took my possessions from me and put me in a cell. They said they wanted to interview me but not until the effects of Ecstasy had worn off completely. I was transferred to Chelmsford police station, where I was kept overnight and interviewed the next day at about noon. Then I was released on bail.

My family did not know anything until Paul rang them from the hospital in the morning. He spoke to my mum to ask if I had arrived home yet. She didn't know what he was talking about. She had not heard the news that day. Dad came straight along to the police station to get me.

I was not so worried about what Dad would say to me. I was far more concerned about Leah and what Paul and Jan would say. I thought Dad might have a go at me, but he just gave me a cuddle. I think he knew I was learning my lesson the hard way. In fact no-one in my family has ever given me a hard time. They have been very sympathetic.

When I eventually arrived home, I telephoned Paul on his mobile phone at the hospital to see how Leah was. I decided to go to the hospital. Paul had told me Leah was unconscious, but I didn't know she couldn't breathe for herself. On the way over I was very nervous. How would Paul, Jan and the family react to me? I wouldn't have blamed them if they didn't want to speak to me, so it was no surprise, when I arrived at the hospital at about 4pm, that they were a bit frosty.

I had been told there would be a lot of machinery in the room, but it was still a shock to see Leah like that. There was nothing I could do except talk to her. I had seen people in films talking to people in comas in the hope they would come around. I played her favourite music to her and I visited her every day while she was in the hospital. I would arrive about 8am and stay until about 10.30pm. Most of the time I found it difficult to stop crying. No-one deserved to be like that. It hurt so much to see Leah lying there and it made it even worse to see Paul and Jan so upset. I felt so guilty.

I think I realised Leah would not recover when there was no response to the reflex tests the doctors were giving her, but I was always hoping she would come out of it, even when they told us they would give her another 24 hours before switching off the machine. I was with Paul and Jan as they said their goodbyes to Leah before her machine was switched off. I was still shocked, crying all the time. As we left the hospital for the last time, Paul took me to one side and asked me to make sure we would never lose contact.

I could not get over Leah's death. I could not go to college, I felt lonely and I could not eat. Paul and Jan were very nice. We would all hug each other and I was telling them how much Leah loved them.

Leah was the first person close to me that had died. It was a shock to see her in the chapel of rest. I had never seen a body before. I'm glad I went to see her there, but I still have nightmares about the stitches on her after the donations. I held her hand, but she was so cold. I'm sure I will always have that image of Leah in my mind.

I cried nearly all the time at the funeral, so much so that it was difficult to read out the poem I had written. My friend's mum had written a similar poem when her father died, so I adapted it for Leah.

Have you ever had a friend that meant the world to you,
*   one you love so very much and miss them like I do;*
Have you ever had the heartache or ever felt the pain,
*   or shed a million tears that drop like falling rain;*
If you've never had that feeling, then pray you never do,
For when God took my friend to Heaven, a part of me went
*   too.*

I still feel guilty because I am still here and Leah has gone. If only I had said to Leah, 'let's not do it tonight'. I've still got my life and a job. Mum and Dad have still got me, but it could just as easily have been their daughter that died.

I didn't have any counselling after Leah's death, although it was offered. At first my friends treated me differently. They closed ranks and were very supportive. I found it hard to get a job because I had been in the newspapers – I was sure it was because everyone thought I was a druggie. Some people are so naïve, they think it could never happen in their family. Their own sons and daughters could be getting up to exactly the same thing. Do they really know what their kids are up to?

Why did we experiment in the first place? Curiosity, I suppose.

We'd heard people saying how good it was but we didn't realise just how dangerous it really was. I didn't fully realise the extent of the danger until Leah became ill and died. That's when it all came out in the newspapers. We knew we might have an allergic reaction to Ecstasy, but we thought that if we didn't, we'd always be all right. Looking back, how naïve we were! To be honest, we didn't think there was that much risk. If we drank enough water, we'd be okay, wouldn't we?

The people we hung around with were not really into drugs, so it wasn't peer pressure that made us experiment, we were just curious. Let's face it, we could have gone into almost any nightclub and someone would have come up to us to see if we wanted anything. They were quite up-front about it. There could easily be an undercover policeman in the club, but that didn't seem to bother them.

Obtaining drugs in nightclubs, at that time, was just about as easy as getting a drink. We never actually bought cannabis. We only had a few puffs of someone else's to see what it was like once. It was like taking a sip of someone's drink to see what it tasted like. I didn't like it at all.

LSD, however, we paid for. If I remember rightly, we paid about £5 for a little square of it. We were in the town centre one night. We approached a man on the street and asked him where we could buy some LSD. We were hoping he was actually a dealer but we didn't know for sure if he was or not. He said he'd go to see someone and come back to us. When he did, he had some for us.

LSD is like a sugar paper square. You place it on your tongue and wait for it to dissolve. After about an hour it makes you feel relaxed. Sometimes you hallucinate – I could see patterns on the ceiling. I felt I could stay up longer and it gave me energy.

Speed is a white powder. You can sprinkle it in a drink of Cola or swallow it without. It tastes horrible, which is why, when we tried it, we took it with a drink. We paid for half a gram of Speed and obtained it in the same way as we had the LSD. If I remember rightly, the going rate at the time for Speed was about £5 a gram. By taking Speed we found we could keep dancing for a long time, but it made us feel paranoid – for instance, we were convinced everyone was staring at us.

We paid about £10 a tablet each time we bought Ecstasy. That was a typical price at the time. When we first took it, we shared the tablet by breaking it in half. This particular one had a dove motif on it, but you can buy them with several different motifs.

We found Ecstasy made us lose all our inhibitions. We felt happy and confident. We could dance and dance for ages. I think Ecstasy is probably the most common recreational drug used and, I have to admit, the effects are enjoyable while they last.

However, as the effects wear off, I found I began to get very tired but could not get to sleep. By the next morning, however, I would feel fine. It's not like going out for a drink one evening and having a hangover the next morning and, whereas drinks in a nightclub are always expensive, many youngsters find it cheaper to pay a tenner for a tablet, have a good time, and wake up the next day feeling OK.

At the trial of the men accused of supplying us with Ecstasy, I was called upon to give evidence. I was so nervous. It was hard to remember the answers to everything I was asked. The defence were trying to make me confused – and it worked! Paul and Jan were there, which made it even worse because, at that time, they did not know Leah and I had been experimenting. But I had to tell the truth. I didn't know how they would react and I didn't get the chance to speak to them afterwards. I couldn't wait to get to a telephone to contact them to see if they were still OK with me. It was a horrible experience.

I hate newspapers. At first I wanted to speak to the newspapers to warn other people about the dangers of drugs. But whatever I said, they seemed to write something else. They pestered me too. When we left the hospital we were followed home. But the worst thing was the night before Leah's machine was switched off. I went into the chapel of rest at the hospital to write a message, a prayer, in the book there for Leah. When I came out, someone from the press must have gone in, copied it out and, the next day, I read it in the newspapers. To me, what I had written was a private thing. After that, I didn't want anything to do with the press.

Some of the newspapers were OK, but there were always going to be one or two that would act in such a way. However, I don't mind doing things for television or things like this for Jan and Paul's book because I know they want to tell people about the good and the bad things about drugs. How else will people ever learn?

Nowadays, I feel very comfortable in Paul and Jan's company. I telephone them every week and I wish I could see more of them. We exchange Christmas presents and visit each other whenever we can. As for William, I love him to bits, so I like to go over to visit him.

I feel so very sorry for Paul and Jan and, of course, for all the distress I have caused my own family. I realise I have behaved stupidly. I didn't need to do drugs. I could have lived with my curiosity. Now, if I thought one of my friends was going to take a drug, I would beg them not to, whatever it was. I could never enjoy the company of anyone if I knew they were on drugs.

I know now that I have grown up an awful lot. I will never, ever, touch drugs again. It is such a shame I had to learn the hard way. That's why I don't want anything to do with people who take drugs. First of all, it makes me nervous and, secondly, there has been so much publicity to warn people of the dangers, so why should they still do it? If there had been as much information available when Leah and I were thinking of doing drugs, we never would have gone ahead. We would never have touched them.

17

A Question of Faith

JANET: Without a doubt, we could not have coped without the help of many of our friends. Two in particular, Rev. Don and Barbara Gordon, have been towers of strength, not only in a practical sense but also in terms of our spiritual and emotional problems. There have been times when we have felt unable to bear the prospect of facing another day, and other times when we have had reason to question our faith, but always Don and Barbara have been there for us. Don describes how they came into our lives.

DON: Before Leah became ill, we hardly knew Paul or Jan, and in fact we did not know Leah at all. We had seen her with Janet in the church for a carol service and, when Paul's mother died over the Christmas period of 1994, we had some contact when I conducted her funeral. Leah attended her grandmother's funeral but those are about the only times I can remember seeing her.

It was not until the Monday morning after Leah's party that I heard about what had happened to her. I heard the news on BBC Essex, our local radio station. Both Barbara and I were anxious to offer our help in whatever way may have been required, but from the news reports it became obvious Jan and Paul had taken up temporary residence at the hospital to be by Leah's side. However, a couple of days later, on the Wednesday morning, I received a telephone call from the sister in charge of intensive care asking me if I would go along to the hospital because the family had asked to see me. I asked the sister when I should come along and she told me I should come as soon as possible.

The unexpectedness of the telephone call had me quite flustered and I hurried to get myself ready. Barbara drove me to the hospital and dropped me off. However, on the journey towards the hospital, both Barbara and I experienced something quite extraordinary. It was a kind of wonderfully calming influence that flowed over us like a warm wave, and this experience was something that was to remain with us over the next few weeks, the significance of which was soon to become apparent.

I had arrived with a completely open mind as to what Jan and Paul wanted me to do. As requested, I reported to the reception desk where I received something of a grilling as to who I was, such was the attention Leah's condition had attracted. I explained I had received a telephone call from the sister in charge and I was shown to the intensive care unit. I was asked to put on a gown and a mask, and then the sister took me through to Leah's bedside. Paul and Jan were there, obviously very strained, but calm. Three or four nurses were also present.

I felt so desperately sorry for them and for Leah but, as a priest, I have learned not to let my own emotions take me over. That is a very important lesson to learn, especially at such times, or when conducting funerals. An emotional priest is not much use to distraught relatives.

Paul was concerned that Leah had never been baptised. 'Do you want me to do it now?' I asked. 'Yes, please,' he said. I asked the sister if she would fetch a finger bowl with some water in it. She returned a few moments later with it and I administered a shortened form of baptism. I then made the sign of the cross on Leah's forehead, said the prayers of commendation, read a psalm and administered the laying on of hands. It was at this precise moment I had the conviction that there was something very, very special happening here. Something worthwhile would come out of this situation.

On leaving the room, the sister told me that Leah's condition was terminal; there was no hope of her recovering. Paul and Jan followed me out to a side wing where the rest of the family were waiting. I tried to assure them of the reality of Christ and of God's love and ultimate control. I was aware that, on a human level, in such a tragedy as this, there was nothing I could do or say that would make any difference. I just wanted to show my willingness to offer the family some moral support.

Five minutes later I rejoined Barbara at our son's house, which was near the hospital. The television was on, and there right in front of me was the photograph of Leah lying in her hospital bed. It was such an eerie feeling. Just a few moments before, I had been standing next to her.

I can quite understand why Paul felt like 'kicking God into touch' when Leah died. There are answers I could have given him, but they would have been of little comfort to him at such a time.

Despite all the sadness and seriousness surrounding the events of those few days, there was at least one incident that I can look back upon with some degree of amusement. Prior to Leah's funeral service, Barbara and I had conducted many television and radio interviews. On one particular occasion, a television crew filmed Barbara and me and our little granddaughter walking towards our church. They wanted me to do something, so I walked up to the lectern.

When the item was eventually screened, there we were walking up to the church and there I was standing at the lectern, but the actual interview was not used. I was then contacted by the television company. Could they screen the communion service in our church the following Sunday? I agreed, but I had to ask them, 'What happened to the interview I recorded with you?' 'Oh, we've still got that,' came the reply, 'but we're keeping it in reserve for Sunday in case your sermon's no good!'

On the Sunday after Leah died, I held the communion service in the village church. There was a considerable congregation and, when the church is so full, I am not always aware of who is actually in the church during the service. But, when it came to the time to give the communion, I looked up and there was Paul, Jan, William and Emily. They had come into the church after the service had started. I administered the laying on of hands to all four of them. That evening, I found myself anxiously sitting on the edge of the settee in front of the television, wondering if my sermon had been judged good enough. Fortunately, it was.

The day of Leah's funeral was quite incredible. I did five radio and six television interviews before 11am. The crowd outside the church was unbelievable and there were press and television cameras everywhere. But, as I described earlier, the warm, calming influence that Barbara and I had experienced on our way to the hospital earlier, stood by us, and I am convinced that feeling helped me considerably that day. For me, the whole ethos of the service and the way everything had slotted into place was a result of the inner calm I was experiencing, even to the point that Leah's funeral address almost wrote itself.

My sermon went along the lines of 'this could be an historic moment. Jan and Paul have shown the courage which has excited the admiration of every right-thinking person. Here we are, an extraordinary mixture of people gathered in this church, police-men, law-makers, clergy, young people, an enormous range of people with such power to be able to do good. Wouldn't it be a wonderful thing if, five or ten years from now, people could look back and say this was a turning point. There would be many setbacks, disappointments and failures, but the tide would have turned.'

Then I prayed that Jan and Paul would have the courage and persistence to carry on what they had begun and for others to give them the support they needed. I greatly admired their courage at the funeral and the way they kept their heads up without sinking into utter despair.

I have to say that neither I nor members of the choir had ever experienced anything quite like the occasion of Leah's funeral, and I should also add that the media behaved quite wonderfully. Despite their huge presence, they were very understanding and were not unnecessarily intrusive.

Imagine my astonishment the following day to find that nearly all the national daily newspapers had printed my sermon at huge length – it was even in *The Times*! It must have made some impression. What I found particularly pleasing about it was that hardly any two newspapers had quoted the same passages of my sermon.

A while after the funeral, Paul and Jan visited us. One of our parishioners had videoed the events of the day and we had obtained a copy. Paul asked if they could watch it with us. By doing so, in our company, I think it helped them to come to terms, to some extent, with their grief.

The following January both Paul and Jan were at a very low ebb. Paul told me they were deeply concerned that interest in their campaign was beginning to fade, that their message was no longer receiving the level of attention of the previous weeks.

I told him to leave it to the Holy Spirit. The Holy Spirit, I explained, does not come to you and just drop you. By coincidence, that night Helen Cousins became ill and went into a coma after taking an Ecstasy tablet. Immediately, because of what had happened to Helen, the media's interest in Paul and Jan's campaign was rekindled overnight. What a a terrible shame it took another near-tragedy to revive the issue.

I suggested they might try to hold some local meetings to discuss the drugs issue in order to maintain the public's awareness. I further suggested they needed an agent, someone to help them arrange the meetings. Very 'tactfully', Paul suggested Barbara and I would fit the bill. As a result, Barbara and I arranged a couple of meetings, one in South Woodham Ferrers and one in Maldon – that was the one where the Australian television crew with the stroppy interviewer turned up. Both meetings were poorly attended but were very useful exercises that helped Paul and Jan develop what was later to prove a very successful presentation formula.

By now both Barbara and I were forming a firm friendship with Paul and Jan and their family, which we value greatly. At first we were very keen to help them in any way we could without pushing in where we were not wanted. They are, after all, a very independent couple and it does not come naturally to them to ask for help.

After a while, however, we felt able to come forward to offer our help. It was an immense joy to me to baptise William and later to be able to confirm both him and Paul. With Jan, they have become towers of strength in our church. In fact Jan, Paul and William have since become members of the choir.

In November 1996 I suggested that Paul and Jan might like to arrange a communion service in memory of Leah. The service was held on the official anniversary of Leah's death. It turned out to be a very meaningful service which gave Paul, Jan, William, Wendy, Emily, and a couple of Leah's friends the opportunity, once again, to come to terms with their grief.

The drugs issue that Paul and Jan have been campaigning against has become like a growing cancer in our society and, I feel, we are all to blame to some degree. We should all be trying to do something about it. We now have a society that feeds on self-gratification and materialism. This is hardly an original observation, but I believe it to be true nonetheless.

Leah's death might be considered by many people to have been a waste, but I am sure, as I was at her bedside in the hospital, that God has taken that tragedy and has used it to good effect. Others have benefited from her death and people are now more aware of the dangers of recreational drugs. There has to be hope for the future.

Paul and Jan have started an initiative and that can be built upon. At first, Barbara and I were very worried that they would burn themselves out. They were so desperate to make as big an impact as they could before the interest died down and the issue was forgotten. They could have had no idea at the time that the issue would command such lasting attention. There is a limit to what just two human beings can do. However, there are now other people beginning to take up the torch – maybe going in slightly different directions – but all with the same aim.

I draw an analogy to the war years. Many soldiers lost their lives in the Battle of Britain in 1940. If it had not been for men like them being prepared to give up their lives for their country, we would not have won the war. In 1945, however, people were celebrating victory, a result of the actions of those men who had given their lives five years previously.

After the trials, I was so delighted to pick up the *Daily Telegraph* to see Paul and Jan referred to in an article as the leading campaigners against Ecstasy. They have stimulated an enormous awareness of this evil. They have made people, including ministers of the crown, sit up and take notice and we feel privileged to have played a part, albeit a small one, in what they have been doing.

It would be ironic, wouldn't it, if, in another 15 years or so, all the forecasts of the effects of Ecstasy – the depressions, psychological problems, liver and kidney failures – were demonstrably proved to be true. It would create a new wave of revulsion in the next generation and the awareness promoted by people like Paul and Jan could, in the end, prove to be the *coup-de-grâce* for this evil trend.

18

A Test of Our Love

JANET: Although our relationship has, fundamentally, not changed, I would say Leah's death, and the events that followed, could have smashed us apart had we not been so close in the first place. The pressures we were under seemed overwhelming. It wasn't just Leah; there were other factors, such as trying to get our boat business off the ground. The drug work was interfering with progress in that direction and Paul was still coming to terms with the death of his mother and his enforced retirement from the police force.

If we had not been so close, we would not have been able to talk things out, but there have been times when we could have ripped each other to pieces. If things had carried on like that we could easily have ended up apart. I don't mean divorce, but just apart until things had died down a bit. We have had to learn a new way of treating each other. Paul and I, when we are upset, react in different ways, with me needing a cuddle and him just needing to be left alone. At first, I felt rejected by him when he needed his solitude. I took it personally. I was wrong, I know that now, but it did cause all manner of upsets. People react differently to stress. There's just no way of telling how it can affect different people.

As far as Paul is concerned, I have nothing but admiration for him. I know I'm biased, because I love him deeply, but every time

I see him interviewed or we give a drug-awareness talk and I watch him having to go through it all again, watching the *Sorted* video and admitting it was Leah's own fault, I am so proud of him. I think back to all that happened in the hospital and afterwards, to a bereaved father, not ashamed to cry. Only people who have been through a similar experience can even hope to know how much he is hurting inside.

He has been congratulated many times for trying to bring awareness of drug dangers to the fore, but I have also had to watch him being verbally attacked face to face. He takes it in his stride, for when you are in a situation like ours you must take the criticism as well, but some incidents really anger me.

Paul is unselfish. If he wasn't, he would have said 'To hell with the lot of you. Ruin your lives if that's what you want to – why should I care?' He is a person who will always listen to another person's point of view. As he says, 'I lay the facts before you. If you don't want to believe them, that's your choice.' It is to prevent the ruination of lives that Paul continues to put himself through such hurt, but it tears at me to see it.

All you patronising writers out there – most of you without children, who only know the fast lane of life, and are interested only in getting yourselves the latest writers' award by being clever and writing of what you perceive to be the latest thinking and trends – I ask you to question your theories in a few years time when, if you are lucky, you have children. Can you honestly say you will be happy if your children are on drugs? Remember it's you that will more likely than not be expected to pick up the pieces.

To all those who claim you cannot possibly know the meaning of life until you have used Ecstasy, I would say what you are experiencing is a false, chemically-induced sensation. It is not spiritual. When you have experienced the birth of your own child, and known what true unselfish love feels like, then have had to stand by helplessly watching him or her die – then you truly know the meaning and value of life.

Since starting ADA, it has been like taking on an extra job. Our house has been taken over by paperwork and the telephone hardly stops ringing. Not that I am complaining. After all, it was our choice to go down that road. It's just that it brings other problems with it. Who is to look after William if we have to go out somewhere to do an interview is just one example.

In January 1997 Tony Bullimore, a lone yachtsman, was trapped underneath the hull of his capsized yacht in freezing conditions in the great Southern Ocean. A huge rescue operation was launched by the Australian Navy. Sailing, of course, is a pastime very close to our own hearts, and you can imagine how pleased we were to hear that he had, after being trapped for a few days, been successfully rescued. But then I saw on the television there was a big PR campaign. His whole family was being offered mega amounts of money, with secretaries and people to answer the telephones. I thought, where was all that for us when Leah died?

At the beginning, if it had not been for certain friends, like Peggy and Hugh Rees taking care of William, my friend Sheila Lloyd helping out, and Andy Hamill doing nothing but answer the telephone for three weeks, what on earth would we have done? Don't get me wrong, I'm not bitter. I was extremely glad that Tony Bullimore was saved. It's just that the very mention of the word 'drug' seems to make people turn away.

Am I angry with Leah? I know Paul admits he has been, but I don't think 'angry' is the right term to describe my feelings. I have, at times, looked at Leah's photograph and asked her 'What on earth did you do that for, Leah? Why did you do such a stupid thing?' No, it's not anger. It's just that I cannot understand what made an intelligent girl like her do something so stupid. I'm sure she cannot have known the full story of what she was doing. It's the lack of information that makes me so sad. That's why we must carry on trying to give youngsters all the facts we have gathered.

It's hard to put into words how much I miss Leah. Most of the time she is in the back of my mind. The time she comes right to the fore is when the whole family is gathered together. That's when it hits us most of all that one of us is missing. I feel so much for Paul. He thinks the world of my girls, but it is not the same as one of your own blood. He realised recently that, if my girls ever decide to get married, their father will be there to give them away. That's something that will never happen for Paul. You don't normally expect your child to die before you, do you?

We often find ourselves reminiscing about Leah. Our passion is sailing and Leah and the girls used to enjoy coming along with us. We own a 29-foot cruiser – hardly the royal yacht *Britannia*, but nice all the same. We started off with a smaller boat but, as the family grew, we bought this one to give us more room. Some people spend their money each year on holidays abroad, but we decided to pay out for a boat that would give the whole family holiday enjoyment year after year.

We have been across to Holland and Belgium in our boat, but usually we were content just to potter up and down the Essex and Suffolk coasts. We found sailing the ultimate cut-off, a source of total relaxation. The wind was free of charge and, unless there was a flat calm, there was never any need to use the engine. On our boating holidays there was no telephone, we could get up when we liked, cook when we liked, go wherever we wanted and went to bed whenever we liked: total freedom. The kids didn't need posh clothes, they could just wear a pair of shorts and their cossies and, if they got covered in sand, it didn't matter.

We have one memory of such a holiday that we always look back upon with great amusement. After one extremely windy day, we were about to pack up. At the end of each day I used to collect the day's washing from the girls, ready to sort it out. We had what we called a 'knicker bucket', a bucket filled with detergent that we used to soak their knickers and socks in overnight.

Cindy and Emily had put their knickers into the bucket and they floated on the top. But, when Leah threw her knickers in, they immediately sank! You can just imagine the comments that caused – I'm certainly not going to repeat them! Leah was almost helpless with laughter and, I will always have the image in my mind of her standing on the pontoon trying to fish out her knickers with a boat hook.

When she was very small, Leah suffered from eczema quite badly. Some of my earliest memories of her was when she was with

Dot and Paul, and Paul was having to apply some cream on to her rashes before putting her nappy back on. I remember the story Dot told me of the time when she and Leah were at a railway station. Leah was just a toddler and her eczema was really troubling her that day. Apparently, in the middle of a crowded platform, Leah had lifted her skirt, pulled down her knickers and had a good scratch!

We have several videos of Leah, but I wish we had more. We treasure them all, but one in particular, filmed when we were on a camping holiday at St Lawrence Bay with Peggy and Hugh and their two girls, is one of my favourites. William was about 18 months old at the time.

Our four girls, plus the other two, put together a little show for us, inspired by the song 'Bright Eyes', which they had learned at the Brownies. Then they all lined up, with one of them standing out at the front, with their thumbs up and singing 'thumbs up, bums out, choo-cha-cha, choo-cha-cha, achoo-cha-cha-cha', then repeated the words with their tongues out and once again with their mouths shut, creating a really strange noise between them. Most Brownies will recognise the song I am talking about. Halfway through, William decided he was going to join in. He toddled up and stood between Cindy and Leah and stood there wriggling his little bum with all the girls giggling at him. It's a brilliant video, one which the whole family really treasures.

Later memories are of the times Leah and Sarah would go upstairs to Leah's room. From downstairs I could hear them chatting happily away. Then Leah would often come downstairs and her head would pop around the door: 'MUUuuum, can we do . . .' or 'Can we go . . .?' I can still hear her saying it to this day. It's times like that I miss so much.

What are my hopes for the future? My main concern is that the drugs issue does not become swept under the carpet. Now it has been highlighted, I hope it will be properly debated. I would also be very happy to take part in that debate, with Paul, but in a more structured way. I would like to be more educated in these matters and possibly even have the opportunity to be able to devote the working part of my life to the issue.

It would also be nice to have more time to spend with the family, perhaps have a holiday. A lot of people have said to us, if everything we have done was to be forgotten tomorrow, would we be on a downer? It could happen. That is why we must not lose sight of our own family.

When we put almost 100 per cent of our efforts into a campaign such as ours, it is easy sometimes to forget we have a partner and family who need us just as much. It's a very fine balance but I would hate all the knowledge we have gained to be wasted. That's one good reason for producing this book. If I go senile overnight, at least this book will preserve some of the knowledge we have accumulated.

Financially, our work with ADA has hit us very hard indeed. We can probably carry on for a while longer, but people don't realise what sort of expenses are involved. They think we get travelling expenses whenever we go to do an interview, or that we are being paid every time we appear on television. It's not like that. We are not paid as if we are actors. Any money we have had donated to us has gone into Leah's Appeal.

From our own pockets we have had to purchase items such as a fax machine, a computer, filing cabinets, and a photocopier. Then we had to add on to the computer because the program could not cope with all we were putting into it. Add to that the costs of postage, printer paper and ink, photocopier paper, paper for the fax machine, an astronomical telephone bill and you can see we get through a fair amount of money. I have also had to cut my working hours down to a part-time basis to fit in work for ADA.

Unfortunately, I cannot afford to give up my nursing work because we need the income to feed the family. On the other hand, we have managed to avoid going into debt. It comes to a stage when we have to be selfish. We cannot allow ADA to bring that sort of pressure on to our family.

PAUL: I'm a keen sea fisherman. Sailing is my life but, since Leah died, we have hardly set foot on our little yacht. We had planned to circumnavigate the world and enjoy ourselves. That won't happen now. Another interest of mine is clay-pigeon shooting but again, following Leah's death, there just hasn't been time. There is so much work I need to do on my boats to get them ready for the Easter and summer seasons, but I see the months slipping by without those jobs being done because of our commitments to ADA.

As Jan says, it is coming to a time when we are going to have to be selfish. If ADA will not allow us enough time to earn a living, eventually it will have to cease – and that would be a terrible scenario to face up to. In 1996, ADA cost us in the region of £5,000 and that is money we could hardly afford. ADA's running costs are a great concern to us. But, recently, I received a letter from a young lady who had been at one of our talks which said, 'Your talk has changed my life for ever. Thank you so much.' It made me think how selfish I am to even consider closing down ADA. When there are people like that, how can I?

We have tried and tried to obtain sponsorship but there is no glory or money to be made from such a deal that would benefit anyone prepared to help us. Not many companies or individuals are prepared to be associated with such a hot potato as the drugs issue: their accountants would tell them it was bad for business.

Each time we do a talk, I have to prepare a new set of notes to suit wherever we are going or whoever we are talking to. It usually takes me three or four days to get a talk just the way we want it. Although our home is hardly a mansion, it is big and we have a lot of animals and ground to look after. Currently, it's falling apart. Initially, when Leah died, I lost all interest in life. When I lost her, I lost life.

When I look back at our diary, about three quarters of it is full of our travels across the UK and Ireland to give talks and to do interviews. Consequently, when we get a rare evening at home, the last thing we feel like doing is decorating. It is getting to the stage where I must discipline myself into drawing up a week's rota with all the jobs down on it, so each day I have a specific task to perform.

I think, if we carry on the way we have been, we could burn

ourselves out. There has been no time for a holiday since Leah died and besides, someone has to look after all our animals. At first, when Leah died, I was so angry with her because of what she had done to the family and to herself. Not only that, there was the stigma attached to a drug-related death. I have educated myself not to feel that way anymore.

I, too, have fond memories of Leah. As a child, she used to love playing family games like Twister, where the players have to entwine themselves around each other to the commands of a rotating arrow. She loved to play Pin the Tail on the Donkey at birthday parties.

I miss the calls of 'DAAaad!. . .' 'What do you want now?' I would say. 'Oh don't be like that' she would reply. I miss the times she would come bounding into our bedroom and sit on the end of our bed and have an hour's discussion. I miss cuddling her when she was feeling sad or lonely. I miss walking along the beach with her. I miss holding her hand. I just miss her so much.

Her death has affected my relationship with Jan. When Leah died, I was still off work sick and my mother had not long died. My whole world was disintegrating around me. Whatever else could happen? Although Jan was a pillar of strength, when I needed my peace and quiet, she would not allow me it. She felt she had to be with me to talk with me and to comfort me.

Jan is just the opposite to me. When she has her bad days, she needs to have a cuddle, to be reassured, whereas I just like to be on my own. That's fine but, if we both have down days at the same time, it just doesn't work out.

Sometimes it has been as if World War Three was breaking out. I know it sounds silly, but it has, at times, been a major stumbling block in our relationship. To be honest, there have been a couple of times when I just wanted to walk out of the door and start afresh.

I know that would not be the answer. I would never have been able to cope without Jan's help, love and guidance, but that's something I've found difficult to tell her. I know Jan needs my love and support just as much as I need hers, it's just that sometimes I wonder if I am strong enough, emotionally, to support her as much as she needs.

I know it is something I have to get over, but I still have such a guilt complex when I go out and enjoy myself. Sometimes I just think enough is enough. I just want to walk out of the door and keep walking. But, quite often, when I feel that way, we receive a letter or a telephone call from some young person saying, 'Thank you, I have been taking Ecstasy but, because of your talk, I'm not going to any more.' That's when reality kicks back in. That's when I feel we must carry on with our message. If we don't, I'm scared that perhaps the topic will die.

I guess, in fact, I'm too scared to stop. That's why we are hoping some other parents who find themselves in the same situation as us can also find it in themselves to come forward to further this campaign. Surely if more of us unite with the same message it can only be a step in the right direction.

We know there are a lot of people who would have preferred it if we had kept our mouths shut. We have received threats and we know there have been people who have the power to do something to keep us out of their way. Have we upset people? You bet, and no doubt we will upset many more people who supply drugs to our youngsters, but we believe we are, at last, beginning to turn the tide. Some youngsters are beginning to take notice of us.

We are playing a small part in cutting the profits of the drug dealers so, of course, we are putting lots of people's backs up. The pro-drug lobby hate us. This came over very strongly when we were in Cardiff. As soon as people get hit in the pocket or are accused of doing something they shouldn't, they try to twist the table to make it seem what they are doing is right and what everyone else is doing is wrong. That is how the pro-drug lobby have reacted towards us. They like to make other people think we haven't a clue what we are talking about, and that the drugs people are taking are perfectly safe.

Have I got faith in humanity? Yes, of course I have. I lost my faith in Christianity when Leah died but, thankfully, with the help of Don's fire-and-brimstone sermons ... Sorry Don (he doesn't really like me describing them like that!) I have it back. I sat in the church feeling so unworthy. I just wanted to walk out. I thought how can I ever renounce God?

Don and I had a long heart to heart and now God is back as my Number One. He still lets me down from time to time, but I'm sure He has a reason for that. Leah had to die for a reason. I may not like that reason, but there was a reason nonetheless. Many may think that's just my way of coping with it. If they do, well fine, but that's the way I want to believe.

Don and his wife Barbara have been so kind to us. They are truly wonderful people. Don is not a bible puncher. He talks to you person to person. He has a wonderful faith and the way that he believes makes you believe as well. My faith is very central to me, although I don't think of God all the time.

I often think of the story of the Pharaoh and the outcast in the church. The outcast would sit at the back and pray before scuttling off out of it, whereas the Pharaoh would stand at the front in full view of all the people to demonstrate how devout he was. The question is, who did God honour the most? Did he honour the Pharaoh for his six hours of worship to show people how faithful he was, or did he honour the outcast who prayed for five minutes in his own way?

I took the story to heart. I believe God is here, there and everywhere. You don't have to be in church to talk to Him or worship Him. Sometimes I think there are more Christians outside the church than there are in it.

I suppose our ultimate goal is unrealisable. We want to stop drugs being used as a recreation. We know that is an impossibility, so we have to look at what can be achieved. We think all the evidence, research and finding should be made readily available for anybody to read so they can make up their own minds. We are finding that very difficult to achieve.

Even in the *British Medical Journal* we have found material that was researched years ago but, because it wasn't topical at the time, wasn't printed. Only following on from what happened to Leah has certain material been printed which is seven years old. A lot of these facts about Ecstasy were already available long before she died.

We want to be able to make people aware of the plus and the minus sides of Ecstasy so they can make an informed choice. If we can do that, we'll be happy. At least then, if they still want to try and kill themselves, that's their choice. We'll have done all that we can.

Symptoms and Recognition

What YOU should know

Paul and I feel it is only right that we share the considerable wealth of knowledge we have acquired since Leah's death with you, the readers. We have made it our business to discover as much as possible about the drugs scene and have spoken to many, many people from different agencies and organisations to that end.

What follows is a distillation of that knowledge, put down here in the hope that it will be of benefit to others. As parents, we have written this part of the book from a parent's perspective, but if you are a young person taking substances, or are thinking of doing so, you owe it to yourself to read on.

Remember, we have found out the hard way – so we feel our experience qualifies us to offer advice in the hope that other parents will not have to go through what we have had to since losing Leah. The next few pages offer advice and information for parents or anyone else who can be bothered to take the time to find out more about the symptoms of drug abuse and the effects of each particular kind of drug.

For those who are still worried, we have included a list of organizations and helplines where confidential and expert advice can be obtained.

It's a must to talk. But it can be the hardest thing to do, particularly if you're faced with a sullen, 'mind-your-own-business' attitude from your child when you try to discover if they are doing drugs. Nevertheless, if you suspect that they are tempted to experiment with drugs, or are already doing so, it's absolutely vital that you make sure that they know exactly what they may be letting themselves in for.

All drugs, whether legal or illegal, are potentially dangerous since they all contain at least one active ingredient which alters, to a greater or lesser degree, your mental and/or physical state. The big difference with prescribed drugs is that you weigh up the advantageous effects this will have on your medical condition against your quality of life without them with your doctor's advice.

People who use drugs for recreational purposes do so in the hope that they will enhance their quality of life by providing an extra 'buzz', or a feeling of relaxation, or that they will blot out that which cannot be faced, all of which can become a habit.

It is important that parents understand that, if their children try a drug, this does not automatically place them in the stereotype 'dirty back-street junkie' category. 'Trying a drug' can mean simply taking a single puff on a joint – and then never again. Yet we should not get in a panic about the situation: nine out of ten kids in this country don't take drugs on a *regular* basis. The danger is that youngsters are given the impression by commercial imagery that everyone is doing it all the time, so if they don't, they're not 'cool'.

Those who *are* doing it will go to a club and pop a pill with no more thought than we do when we go to the pub for a pint and a smoke. The difference is that most adults know for sure that alcohol and tobacco are potentially harmful and addictive. We can make a truly informed choice about drinking and smoking. That many of us don't make a very sensible choice is beside the point: at least we are aware of the dangers of our actions.

The immorality of our kids' situation is that the huge commercial world which our kids have to face has made it its business to let them know all about the enjoyable feelings and the 'cool' side of drug taking, but little about the dangers which are known, even though those making profit from their sale in all kinds of ways will have to think otherwise, or they get lost in a load of rubbish statistics about eating peanuts or getting struck by lightning to try and show how little chance there is of dying from taking an illegal drug.

The fact remains that approximately 2,500 people die from illegal drug misuse each year in England and Wales alone. (UK Parliamentary answers and questions 1994).

Everyone shies away from the longer-term possibilities, burying it in a 'we don't know for sure' attitude or 'monkeys' brains are different from ours, anyway' answer. We have exactly the same scenario as we had 40 years ago with tobacco – the users finding an excuse for it, the commercial world marketing it in any way they could to sell it; the medical researchers being told they were daft because they only tested it on animals, so 'their results were inconclusive'; and the parliament of the time sticking its head in the sand, each party hoping they wouldn't be in power if the lid came off and they had to finance the NHS bill to treat all the people suffering these long-term effects WHICH DON'T EXIST IF YOU IGNORE THEM LONG ENOUGH!

And look where we are now – over 111,000 people die prematurely from tobacco-related illnesses each year in Britain (HEA 1996) – Fact.

A third of deaths in the under 45 age group are from alcohol-related diseases – Fact.

These statistics alone must be the greatest advert for not legislating all these other *recreational* drugs! It really has solved all our problems with tobacco and alcohol, hasn't it? The manufacturers and retailers go on making the money, and the Government goes on collecting revenues – because money and business are more important than people.

So, bearing all of this in mind, it is our duty as parents to talk to our kids, with credibility, about this issue, before profit makers do. But let's get this into perspective – *not everyone's doing it* – it's just the minority who shout the loudest for their rights. However, the chances are that your child will be *offered* drugs, and they need to be armed with facts and self-esteem to refuse, if that is their choice.

In order to be able to make an *informed* choice your kids need access to ALL the facts, not have them swept under the carpet and hope drugs go away, or sanitised by well-meaning adults; and parents have to accept that their kids can get an enjoyable feeling from these substances, otherwise millions of kids wouldn't be wasting their money every weekend. Kids are under great pressure to be liked; to be seen as individual; to fit in with their friends; to look right; to feel good about themselves. If they have problems they may want to talk about them, but often they won't choose their parents to talk to. It may be they don't feel comfortable talking to them, either because 'they won't understand anyway', or because they'll 'go up the wall'. Think back: did you dare to mention *sex* to your mum? If they do feel they can talk to you, it's practically guaranteed they will choose a time when you are busy, or 'not in the mood'. Make time!

There are no easy answers, but bear in mind the following:

1   Talk *with* your children not *to* them, and try to let them feel able to talk about everything going on in their lives. Remember, you were young once. Think back: were you such an angel?
2   Do everything you can within the family to prevent boredom. Encourage hobbies, interests and social activities. Give your children time; it doesn't cost money to be there for them. Don't complain if you have to miss an episode of *Neighbours* to pick them up after a late school activity.
3   Try not to speak or act hastily, doing or saying things you may regret later. (Not always easy!)
4   Learn as much as you can about what interests and involves your children and their friends.
5   Find out about the drugs-education programme at your childrens' school, so that you can talk about what they are learning. A decent drugs policy does not mean that your child's school has a big drugs problem; it means that the head and the governors are being sensible and realistic.
6   Make it known to your children that there is no problem which cannot be sorted out; you may not understand how they could have got into a situation, but you will support them to face it.
7   Remember, they are individuals. They have a right to their

views as well. Think back to when you were convinced that nobody understood or cared about *your* point of view because of your age, and how that felt. Take an interest in their problems and they will be much more likely to confide in you. You might then be able to influence whether or not they experiment with drugs.

8 Take note of the example you are setting them. The way they see you using alcohol, tobacco and medicinal drugs may greatly influence them. It gives them signals about how you regard drugs. If they see you abusing your acceptable drugs, why shouldn't they abuse theirs? If you are hooked on yours and are unhappy about it, tell them so. Don't be frightened to admit that you are dependent on your fags or beer – and what a waste of money and health it has been. Otherwise they will just copy you, after all, great-granddad drank five pints, smoked 40 fags a day and lived to the age of 90, and he had no ill effects, did he? Or did he? Maybe those effects just were not recognised or talked about in his time. What about those around him? Did his habits affect them?

9 Show, and say, you care. Your children should be valued and cared for. LOVE COSTS NOTHING!

How do you know if your child is doing drugs?

It's a hard thing to pick out, especially if the use is occasional, and the big problem is that many of the signs match those of adolescence anyway. However, the following may be tell-tale signs.

· Sudden and marked changes of mood – happy and alert one moment, sullen and moody the next. Unusual irritability or aggression. Loss of interest in their appearance and, sometimes, hygiene – 'a different person' who bites your head off if you open your mouth.
· Loss of appetite, restlessness, sleeplessness; or a craving for sweet things when they come home after a night out: 'the munchies' (sometimes a sign of cannabis use).

- Bouts of drowsiness or unexplained tiredness.
- Loss of interest in hobbies, sport, and not wanting to join in any more.
- Friends dropped and replaced by new ones, when they seemed to get on well with the old ones.
- Unexplained absences from school, college or workplace, and school work suddenly going downhill for no apparent reason.
- Evidence of lying, or furtive or generally 'out-of-character' behaviour.
- Excessive spending of money, with no goods to show for it.
- Unexplained 'loss' of money or possessions, particularly from the home.
- Unfamiliar smells or stains on skin and clothing, or around the house.
- Sores or rashes, especially on the mouth and nose.
- Unusual capsules, tablets, or items such as plastic bags or tin foil wrappers.

You know your child better than anyone, so you will notice changes in behaviour. If you do discover that your child is using drugs or solvents, don't panic. Stay calm in order to decide the best way to tackle it. You will need answers to some basic questions from your child in order to find an explanation for what you have noticed, but avoid asking them aggressively or in a way which creates an instant argument. Be sure of your facts, and don't jump to over-hasty conclusions.

If the occasion was a one-off you may simply need to discuss it with them. Be firm, consistent and caring, but make it clear that you don't approve of what they have done. They may never intend to try drugs again, or they may be experimenting. They may have enjoyed the feeling the drug gave them, and the feeling of taking risks. Give your child some of the reasons why it's a bad idea to do drugs:

- That it's illegal and could lead to trouble with the police, for you and them.

- That drug taking could affect their health both now and in the future.
- That it could affect their chances of doing as well as possible in their exams and career and that their chances of working abroad or getting a job could be jeopardised.

Try to discover *why* your child has taken drugs. Drug use often needs to be seen in the context of overall situations such as family or personal relationships, progress at school, college or work, and what their friends are doing. Frequent misuse can make them dependent on the drug, while occasional use gives the body and the mind a better chance to recover.

If your child's health or behaviour shows that they are taking drugs regularly you should take further action. Don't be afraid to intervene: you are helping them in the long run. Your child will need your support, whatever the circumstances. Build on your relationship; show them that you love and care for them, no matter how much you disagree with what they have done.

DON'T BE FRIGHTENED TO GO AND SEEK HELP! It will stop you feeling panicky and help you feel more in control. This is not a question of bringing a stigma on your family, it is a question of helping your child, just as you would seek a doctor's advice if he or she were ill. Ask for help from family and friends, and professionals.

The telephone numbers of local helplines are often listed in local directories, newspapers, and local radio stations may have them. National helplines are listed at the back of this book. Most of them can put you in touch with local branches.

Be realistic. If your child has been taking drugs regularly they are not going to be able to suddenly stop. They may be psychologically hooked, and it doesn't work like that. Any improvement will be gradual. There will be slip-ups, when your back-up will be vital.

You will need support as well – and remember, it's not your fault! With many kids doing drugs is simply a passing phase, not a reaction to deep personal problems or a rejection of your way of life.

The Law

The two main laws concerning drugs in the UK are the Medicines Act and the Misuse of Drugs Act.

The Medicines Act controls the way medicines are made and supplied. The Misuse of Drugs Act bans the non-medical use of certain drugs.

The Misuse of Drugs Act places banned drugs in different classes: A, B and C. The penalties for offences involving a drug depend on the class it is in, and will also vary according to individual circumstances.

Class A drugs carry the highest penalties: a maximum of 7 years for possession, and life imprisonment for dealing. Class B drugs carry a maximum penalty of 5 years for possession, and 14 years for dealing.

First offenders who are charged with possessing drugs for their own use may be only cautioned or fined – but *even a caution carries a criminal record, with all that that entails.*

Regular offenders – people selling drugs or drug smugglers – can be sentenced to life imprisonment for trafficking. In England and Wales children from 10 to 16 years of age are dealt with by Juvenile Courts, which can fine the parents or put the offender in detention.

It is an offence to allow anyone on your premises to produce, give away, or sell illegal drugs.

It is an offence even to offer to supply such drugs free of charge.

Consequently, if a parent knows that their child is sharing drugs with a friend in their house and does nothing to stop it, the parent has committed an offence. This includes even such things as passing a joint between a group of friends. Allowing the smoking of cannabis in your home is also an offence.

To stop someone committing an offence with a drug, you can either destroy the drug or hand it over to the police.

Common Recreational Drugs

Amphetamine Sulphate

Also known as 'speed', 'whiz', 'billy', 'uppers', 'sulphate'.

What it does for *you*
Stimulates the nervous system, speeds up breathing and heart rate. It keeps you awake, energetic, self-confident and exhilarated for several hours. Also used to suppress the appetite, and was used in slimming pills in years gone by.

Signs of abuse
The user may appear unusually energetic and cheerful, and excessively talkative while under the influence of the drug. Restlessness and agitation are also characteristic.

There is a lack of interest in food, and it causes unusual sleeping patterns. Regular users may use the drug to stay awake for two to three nights at a stretch, then sleep for up to 48 hours. Mood swings are common. The regular user often looks pale and drawn, with dark rimmed eyes, is constantly fidgety, and frequently sniffing.

How is it sold
It is sold in a paper wrap as a white or greyish powder, which is usually sniffed or 'snorted', or as a tablet swallowed with a drink. Can be used for injection.

As a powder or tablet amphetamine is a Class B drug. If prepared for injection it becomes Class A. At around £10 a gram, the purity of what is sold can be as low as 5%.

The effects described last for several hours, so it is often used at all-night parties and clubs. But the energy it appears to give the user is a short-term 'high'; as it wears off, users often feel exhausted, depressed and anxious.

Even at low doses, speed can cause mood swings, temper tantrums, irritability and restlessness, depression and fatigue. At high doses it may cause shaking, sweating, anxiety, headaches, palpitations and chest pain.

After a period of repeated use, amphetamines disrupt eating and sleeping patterns so much that people become run down and less able to cope with everyday pressures, as well as becoming more vulnerable to infections and other illnesses, frequently with weight loss and constipation.

A result of these effects is that some amphetamine users start to take higher and higher doses of the drug in an attempt to feel as good as they did at the beginning. This not only increases the negative effects but can create a tolerance to the drug, and users become psychologically dependent on the effects of the drug. This can lead them on to 'harder' drugs.

They can experience episodes of aggression and paranoia and, in some people, this leads to serious mental health problems. Severe depression and suicide are associated with sudden withdrawal, and so it is *VITAL* to seek professional help if you have become dependent on the drug.

While most young users take amphetamines by snorting the powder, as amounts increase some users start to inject the drug, which brings all the risks associated with overdoses, damage to the veins and dangers of infections such as hepatitis and HIV.

Because of its low price and easy availability, amphetamine sulphate is one of the most frequently used stimulant drugs in this country.

Cannabis

Indian hemp, derived from the *Cannabis sativa* plant. Also known as 'grass', 'pot', 'dope', 'weed', 'hash', 'ganja', 'shit', 'blow', 'wacky baccy'. There is also a newer form called 'skunk' which is much stronger than the others, and so called because it does literally stink! Cannabis averages 5% tetrahydrocannibal (THC), skunk 9–30%. THC is the active mind-altering ingredient in cannabis. It is a depressant and hallucinogenic.

What it does for *you*
It takes effect in seven seconds. It promotes a feeling of relaxation and well-being, enhances sounds and visual perceptions, and increases talkativeness. It increases the appetite. Some people feel no effect at all. The effects last for one to three hours after smoking, and up to 12 hours or longer after it is eaten. However, presence is detectable in urine samples for many weeks.

Signs of abuse
The user may appear unusually talkative, relaxed, chatty, giggly or drunk while under its effects. There is a very distinctive herbal smell, that may hang on the hair and clothes of users or their non-using companions.

The pupils of the eyes dilate (enlarge) initially, then become 'pin-pricks'.

Users who come home after doing cannabis may have 'the munchies': they will raid the larder for food, usually sweet things like Mars bars, and will eat them as quickly as possible. Sometimes it induces a feeling of nausea, known as 'the whiteys'.

King-size Rizla papers, sometimes along with tobacco, often with cardboard tubes known as 'roaches', used as cooling filters, may be found; pipes, cans or bottles are adapted for inhalation use.

How it is sold
Cannabis can be bought in the form of 'herbal' consisting of dried leaves, stalks and seeds, known as marihuana or 'grass', or as a solid

brown lump of resin, known as 'hashish' or 'hash'. Both forms are usually mixed with tobacco and smoked in a 'joint', 'reefer', or 'spliff' made with cigarette papers and a cardboard filter, or smoked in a pipe. Alternatively, a portion of cannabis may be placed between two hot knives under a broken bottle or jar, and the resulting fumes breathed into the lungs.

Both forms can also be brewed into a drink, made into 'hash cakes', or eaten with food. Herbal cannabis can be smoked on its own.

Cannabis can also be bought in oil form, needing only the amount you get on the head of a pin when dipped into the oil to make a joint.

Cannabis leaf and resin are Class 'B' drugs; it is illegal to possess, sell or give them away. Cannabis oil is a Class A drug.

Cannabis is relatively cheap. For £10 enough joints can be made to last five or six people an evening. An ounce of cannabis costs about £100; the typical user spends £25 to £50 a week on it.

Under the influence of the drug, short-term memory loss can occur, and physical co-ordination is disrupted. Some users also suffer a loss of the sense of time, confusion, and emotional distress, sometimes with hallucinations. Those taking it when they feel depressed may find that unpleasant feelings such as paranoia or depression are heightened.

There are also immediate risks which young people need to be aware of. The drug lowers inhibitions and can make unprotected sex more likely.

There is also an increased risk of accidents while driving because normal reflexes are slowed down.

In the long term cannabis smoking, like tobacco smoking, increases the risk of bronchitis and lung cancer. There is also now evidence that cannabis causes certain specific cancers in its own right, particularly in the head and neck region. Long-term memory loss is also a problem.

Regular users may become apathetic and lethargic, and neglect their work or studies and their personal appearance. In susceptible people, heavy use may trigger a temporary psychiatric disturbance, and schizophrenia can be precipitated.

Many people already with mental health problems smoke cannabis, having been convinced that it will make them relax. It actually makes their condition worse, and is often incompatible with their prescribed drugs.

Problems arise from a mental need for the drug's effect and regular users can develop dependence. This is evident now in countries such as Holland where cannabis use has been 'accepted' for some time. There are over 77,000 admissions a year to treatment programs for cannabis use recorded, and annually almost 8,000 people require emergency hospital care. (National Institute on Drug Abuse, USA)

There is also now increasing evidence, much of it from users themselves, that cannabis *does* lead to experimentation with other drugs. This usually happens when the 'buzz' from cannabis is no longer enough, or users find it impossible to relax without some form of drug.

People with heart disorders should not use cannabis, as it may lower blood pressure and increases heart rate.

The Social Problem

Cannabis is the most commonly used illegal drug in the UK. The pro-drug lobby want the government to declare its possession and use legal. It's the one the pro-drug lobby want to begin their legalisation plan with! For these reasons, and because the label *'herbal'* seems to con many people into thinking it is a harmless little weed, we feel the findings of some of the latest research should be briefly outlined here to dispel some myths.

The toxic properties of cannabis smoke are grossly underestimated. To get technical, its smoke contains carbon monoxide, acetaldehyde, naphthalene, and carcinogens (cancer-causing agents) – all nasties – and has a far higher tar content than tobacco, which is why it burns hotter. It's a *super fag!*

Arguments for its use in the medicinal field have been put forward. Its active ingredient, THC, is already in use. It is synthetically produced in pill form, and is known as Marinol in the USA and Nabilone in the UK. It is used as an anti-emetic (prevents nausea and vomiting) for patients on anti-cancer drugs. It is no less therapeutic than inhaling THC in smoke form, but minus the dangers; and smoke will induce sickness! In pill form the effects are longer lasting and more constant and controllable.

As with all medicines, a warning is put on the label for the benefit of doctors prescribing it. It reads:

Warning!
THC encourages both physical and psychological dependence and is highly abusable. It causes mood changes, loss of memory, psychosis, impairment of co-ordination and perception and complicates pregnancy.

This is a pharmaceutically-based direct warning to the medical profession – not a maybe!

It is sometimes argued that cannabis smoking relieves pain. *Research so far seems to show that THC increases the perception of pain.* Cannabis is NOT an analgesic (pain killer).

Apart from all this medical research evidence, it concerns us greatly that so many addicted users of a variety of drugs have stated both to us and to other agencies that cannabis was the drug they started with.

One prisoner, doing time for crimes committed to feed his habit, wrote to us: 'I went from cannabis to crack in two years. You go through them all – start with joints, then you're using it just to sleep, but don't get a buzz, so you do a bit of speed, a few 'E's, then use bigger gear to come down on. Then you get a mind blower, and you can't do without it. You need more and more, and crack is the ultimate high. Don't ever let anyone tell you cannabis is harmless. It gets you into drugs.'

He begged us to make this known, so that's what we're doing.

Cocaine

A narcotic derived from the leaves of the coca plant (*Erythroxylon coca*). Also known to users as 'coke', 'charlie', 'snow', 'nose candy'.

What it does for *you*
A powerful stimulant which creates a feeling of well-being and elation, decreased appetite and increased confidence. It confers an indifference to pain (it is still used as a local anaesthetic) and over-comes tiredness.

Signs of abuse
While under its influence, the pupils of the eyes dilate and the user may tremble and sweat. The heart rate and blood pressure increase.

The user shows little interest in food, but seems unusually exuberant and energetic. He may suffer insomnia and become exhausted due to lack of sleep. He may constantly be sniffing. Heavy regular use leads to disturbed patterns of sleeping and eating, with agitation, mood swings and aggressive suspiciousness of other people.

How it is sold
Cocaine is sold as a white powder, which is usually chopped up, divided in lines on a mirror then sniffed up the nose through a tube. Sometimes it is injected, or it may be processed into a form which can be smoked, known as *'freebasing'*.

Cocaine is a Class A drug, illegal to possess, sell, or give away.

It is a stimulant which, in moderate doses, overcomes fatigue and induces feelings of confidence and elation – hence it became the 'yuppie' drug. The problem is that users become dependent on these effects, and are often tempted to increase the dose and the frequency with which they take it.

Owing to its appetite-reducing effects, it is often used by fashion models seeking the desired anorexic appearance, and by people in high-pressure jobs in order to keep on top of things, to cover up the 'burn-out'. Large doses lead to agitation, anxiety and paranoia, with hallucinations and violent behaviour.

In the long term, repeated sniffing can lead to damage to the membranes lining the nose, and eventually the destruction of the septum (the structure separating the nostrils) so that you no longer have two passages leading from your nostrils. Users lose weight, and become increasingly anxious, restless and paranoid, with psychosis. Very large doses can lead to convulsions and death due to heart failure.

One of the biggest problems with cocaine is that even if a user or those near to him realise that he/she has a problem, they feel full of confidence when on the drug, and become paranoid about going to a drug agency or a doctor for help for fear of losing that boost to their lives.

N.B. *If a user has to undergo a general anaesthetic for any reason, it is essential that he tells the anaesthetist of his/her habit, however small.*

Crack

Also known as 'rock', 'wash', 'stone'. Crack is cocaine that has been treated with chemicals and processed into the form of small crystals to make it more easily smoked and more quickly absorbed. It is highly addictive.

The effects are immediate, far more intense and powerful than those of untreated cocaine; but short-lived, lasting only a few minutes, and leaving an immediate craving for more. This craving is so intense that the user will do anything to obtain additional supplies. Some heavy users use heroin to help them come down from such an intense 'high'.

Long-term use leads to coughing up black phlegm, wheezing, chest pains and permanent lung damage, as well as damage to the lips, tongue and throat from the hot fumes.

Mental deterioration is rapid, with personality changes, withdrawal from society, and violent, unpredictable behaviour. Attempts at suicide often occur, as do casualties from abnormal heart rhythms, high blood pressure, strokes and death.

Ecstasy

Methyldioxymethamphetamine (MDMA). Also known as 'doves', 'apples', 'eves', 'rhubarb & custard', 'strawberry milkshakes', 'white lightnings', 'sitting duck', 'XTC', 'adam', 'diamonds', 'yellow callies', and at least a hundred other nicknames, including, inevitably, 'Leahs'.

What it does for you
The effects are a mixture of stimulant and hallucinogen. Users feel happy, energetic and want to dance all night (from the amphetamine in it); they want to talk to each other, and touch each other (hence the rise in sales of 'nice to touch' fabrics in the fashion scene). It reduces inhibitions and makes you feel more sexy but men may find the effects impair their sexual performance. You feel like you love everything and everyone. Users have heightened perception of colours and sounds.

Signs of abuse
While under the influence of the drug, the pupils of the eyes dilate widely, so much so that hardly any iris is visible. Users will talk nineteen to the dozen.

People intending to take 'E' while they are out will often take a change of clothes, cool and dance style, because they sweat so much when it takes effect. Sometimes they have whistles, or masks to inhale Vick, which is said to heighten the effects of E.

They will often stay out all night, and spend the next day 'out of it', with a depressive state of mind during the week when not doing the drug. They can't wait 'til the next weekend, when they can do it again; consequently, what they do during the week becomes less important.

How it is sold
Ecstasy comes in capsules of different colours, often pink or pastel shades, or twin-coloured. It also comes in tablet form, which have

different motifs on them, such as an imprint of a dove or of an apple with a bite taken out. Price is dependent on the area you live; they can be as little as £3.50 and as much as £12 each.

Ecstasy is a Class A drug in all forms, as is MDEA – an almost identical drug with a slightly different chemical structure but with exactly the same effects.

This class of so-called 'recreational' drugs are psychiatric drugs which, because of the 'loved-up' feeling they give you, found their way out on to the streets, but because of their side effects, they have been banned for medical use in every country except Switzerland.

MDMA started life as MDA (methyldioxyamphetamine). Until in the 1960s the so-called 'godfather' of Ecstasy, Alexander Shulgin, played with it in his garden 'laboratory' and added the extra -meth- to create MDMA. Shulgin claims he created it for psychiatric use but in the 1980s it found its way on to the streets.

One interesting aspect of MDMA is that it stimulates the brain in such a way that your movements become repetitive. You are capable of coping with only six to eight movements at any one time and, coincidentally, at the same time as MDMA found its way on the streets, 'dance' music was born. By 'dance' music we mean the constant repetitive beat ('Escort' music some people call it) made famous by the McDonalds advert ('If you can't afford a stereo, get a mate to sit in the back of your car and bang on the sides'). The beat fits perfectly with the drug; so the question is posed – which came first, Ecstasy on the street or the dance music?

So, we set the scene for Ecstasy; the beat, the skimpy dance fashions made from tactile materials with added logos like XTC, the psychedelic images which are now found in magazines, on book covers, advertising, and chill-out areas. A whole money-making commercial scene, sold to our youngsters in such a way that they dare not opt out from taking part for fear of not 'being cool'.

As soon as E takes effect, after about half an hour, the body temperature rises rapidly by as much as 2–3°. The heart rate can double, with a consequent sharp rise in blood pressure. The muscles tense, particularly in the jaw, and users often grind their teeth. E affects the brain's ability to control water balance within the body in a complicated process resulting in kidney failure, so that you cannot pass urine.

There have been many casualties from the overheating effects of Ecstasy. The first few recorded deaths were put down to heat-stroke and dehydration caused by this dramatic rise in body temperature. Clubbers were dancing for hours on end, in what is already a hot atmosphere.

After the first batch of deaths from heat-stroke, promoters of E then started putting out the information that to counteract these effects you should drink a lot of water. As usual commercial enterprises latched on to this. Water taps in clubs were turned off so that clubbers had to buy their water, sometimes at £2–3 for a small bottle. If they could afford it, this seemed the answer to a clubber's dream, until casualties and deaths occurred when people drank litres and litres of water. Because they couldn't wee, the brain soaked up the excess water, causing irreparable damage and often death. It didn't take much fluid for this to happen.

Contrary to what you may have heard or read, Leah did not drink gallons of water. She had had a few glasses of Coke, but this was sufficient for her brain to swell.

So, 'harm-reduction' was born. Users were told to drink a pint of water sipped over an hour, and to 'chill out'. This may be all right if, while under the influence of the drug, you know and remember what you are doing. Unfortunately most users feel very thirsty, but don't know how much they have had.

But dehydration is more complicated than just not drinking enough. Users were told they must replace body salts to redress the balance of electrolytes in the body's chemical processes. Once again the commercial world latched on. Isotonic drinks (the type sold to be drunk after exercise) suddenly doubled in price in clubs, and portions of melon and suchlike were sold.

During this period we were assured: 'Ecstasy is safe. There have only been 50 deaths' – as if 50 deaths was acceptable. Nobody bothered to point out that the magic number of 50 came from coroners' verdicts who had actually recorded the death as being drug related. Nobody mentioned all the families spared the stigma of a drug-related death verdict by a kind coroner in cases where the deceased had been admitted to hospital after taking E, had died a few days or weeks later from liver or kidney failure, or haemorrhages particularly from the brain and lungs, and the cause of death was recorded on the death certificate as organ failure. Nobody mentioned all the near-misses who were in ITUs and survived, some with permanent disabilities. Nobody mentioned all the casualties regularly taken to accident and emergency departments every week, some with unexplained symptoms which casualty officers are now waking up to.

Everyone was trying to find excuses for taking the drug. Few would come straight out and say it was an unsafe thing to do. Can you imagine the outcry if we had all these advised precautions, deaths and casualties attributed to a prescribed drug? It would be banned – end of story. Ecstasy WAS banned for medicinal use for that reason, and yet it seems to be accepted that our kids can go ahead and harm themselves for recreation! Just so long as the entrepreneurs don't lose money, and the people with power don't have to spend too much time or money, or stick their necks out to tackle the problem *'cos it'll never happen to them or their kids, will it? So why should they worry?*

More worrying than the danger of immediate harm are the long-term effects. When researchers first noticed these and started collating the evidence, the pro-E lobby told them they were scare-mongering. The researchers were pointing out the effects that Ecstasy has on the chemical seratonin in the brain, and the damage done to the receptors passing messages on via this chemical. Seratonin is a neurotransmitter, a chemical in the brain which conducts messages between nerve endings, bridging the gap so that messages get through to all parts of the body. When you take Ecstasy, seratonin is released in floods (that's what gives you the loved up feeling) but this excessive amount damages the nerve endings, and the seratonin is lost, whereas normally it would be reabsorbed for future use.

In medical terms, Ecstasy is most definitely neurotoxic; neuro – to do with the nervous system, toxic meaning poisonous. Damage occurs each time you take the drug, but the effects are not always detected immediately. People notice a user's personality slowly changing, and spells of depression increase. Paranoia can set in, very like the effects of taking pure amphetamine.

One psychiatric unit in Wales is on record as stating that of every 50 patients admitted, 35 are Ecstasy psychotics, sometimes pacing the ward like caged animals. Dr. John Henry at Guy's Hospital, the consultant in toxicology, is certain that a proportion of Ecstasy users will become suicidally depressed in the years to come, and that that proportion could be as high as 50% of users. Dr. Henry's findings on all animals tested so far have been the same, and he states that he can see no reason to believe they will be any different in humans.

In 1996 the suicide rate in the 15–24 age range trebled. Has Ecstasy played a significant role here? But still the commercial world encourages its use.

Users are told it is not addictive. True, it is not physically addictive, but it is unquestionably psychologically addictive. Users start on one tablet. This is fine for a few weeks, then one isn't enough to give a buzz, so they take two, then three, and so on. We have met users doing 10 or 12 at a weekend, some over four days, and they are a mess. Ex-users will tell you that they still experience psychological symptoms, and they are the *real experts.*.

When you start taking this sort of dosage, you often get into the habit of taking some other drug to come down on, to ease the symptoms. Drugs like Temazepam have been used, and heroin smoked. The danger of addiction does not need to be pointed out. Smoke heroin and you get hooked.

We can't understand why pop groups who say they take drugs and write songs about it are hailed as heroes. Authors who write pro-drug books have venue owners queuing up to launch their books in their premises; alternative comedians crack jokes about addiction and people roar with laughter – human nature has always been to laugh at things it can't fully understand. Club owners who claim to want their clubs drug-free employ licensed security staff, and turn a blind eye. Or perhaps we can understand – it's called money!

MPs play at tackling it; some judges don't use the full powers they have; and civil rights people say we can't crack down 'because it's unfair on the users'. What about the non-users? What about their right to go out and not have drugs shoved in their face? They shouldn't have to be figuring out *how* they can say no – IT'S THEIR RIGHT ANYWAY!

Heroin

(Diamorphine) Comes from the white milk derived from the unripe seed capsules of the opium poppy (*Papaver somniferum*). Commonly known as 'smack', 'junk', 'H', 'scag', 'brown', 'horse', 'stuff'.

What it does for *you*
Heroin is a depressant which produces a feeling of drowsy contentment and warmth. Highly addictive.

Signs of abuse
Heroin gives the user a drunken and drowsy appearance, with pinpoint pupils. Users neglect their personal appearance, lose weight and their appetites, and show no interest in their previous hobbies and social activities. Their personalities change, and their behaviour becomes furtive.

How it is sold
When pure, heroin is a white powder. When impure, it is a brown speckled powder. Heroin contains morphine and codeine, both powerful painkillers.

On the street heroin can be cut with all sorts of other substances, such as talcum powder, glucose, caffeine, quinine and flour.

Heroin is a Class A drug. It can be either sniffed, smoked, or injected. Its price can vary enormously from area to area, depending on local demand, or on how much has been stock-piled due to the popularity of other, cheaper drugs.

Users get hooked on heroin for different reasons. Some are on such high doses of other recreational drugs that they smoke heroin to ease the unpleasant come-downs from these. Others, became hooked when manufacturers started coating drugs such as Ecstasy with heroin. Most simply need a bigger high than the ones they are already getting from other drugs.

First-time users often feel sick, and vomit. Tolerance to the effects of this drug builds up quickly, and it is not long before the user needs larger and larger amounts to 'chase the dragon' of that first feeling. With higher doses comes increased drowsiness, often leading to coma and death when the nervous system is depressed so much that breathing stops.

Overdosing is a real danger, particularly as the user never knows the purity of the stuff he has bought. Prolonged use leads to constipation, lack of sexual drive, disruption of menstrual periods, and poor eating habits, with personal neglect leading to general ill-health. The user's lifestyle revolves around its use.

Many of the substances that heroin is cut with can damage blood vessels and clog the lungs. Along with this goes the risk of contracting infections such as hepatitis A, B and C, HIV and syphilis from unclean or shared needles, and the risk of abscesses at the injection sites.

After only a few weeks of use, sudden withdrawal produces flu-like symptoms 6–24 hours after the last dose – hot and cold sweats, runny nose and eyes, aches, shaking, sleeplessness, anxiety, vomiting and diarrhoea with muscle spasms and stomach cramps. This is 'going cold turkey', and the effects are at their worse 48–72 hours after withdrawal, and fade away after 7 to 10 days.

The biggest problem then comes – how to fight the psychological craving for heroin. The craving can be so strong that an addict may undergo treatment of different types several times, and still not be able to resist using it again.

L.S.D.

Lysergic acid diethylamide. A Class A drug, commonly known as 'acid', 'haze', 'trips', 'microdots', 'tab', 'dots', 'blotters'.

What it does for *you*
A 'trip' makes the user hallucinate. It takes effect in 30 to 60 minutes.

Initially there is a feeling of dizziness, restlessness, and shivery coldness. There is uncontrollable laughing. The user will see things that aren't there, or have distorted vision often for as long as 8 to 12 hours. The user's sense of time, place, sound and colour get all mixed up. People say they can 'see sounds' or 'feel colours'. These are just distortions. True hallucinations are rare.

Signs of abuse
Users under the influence of LSD rarely show outward signs of its effects. Sometimes they may seem over-excited, withdrawn or confused. They may talk of what they are seeing, which may sound like nonsense to the non-user. If they are having a bad trip, they may be very disturbed emotionally.

How it is sold
Acid is sold on small squares of blotting paper, no bigger than a quarter of a postage stamp in size. Each square will have a distinctive picture on it, such as a strawberry, a smiley face, Superman, or a rising sun. Different pictures are chosen to make them attractive to sell, and these pictures can tell you the age of a tab, depending which one was the popular 'brand' at that time. LSD can also be obtained in tablet or capsule form, sold on gelatine sheets or sugar cubes.

Tabs can be as cheap as £1.50 each. They are put on to the tongue, or under the eyelid, where the LSD can be absorbed easily.

Tabs are made by printing the sheet with the squares, and then either spraying on the liquid solution, or dipping the sheet in, as in photographic developing, and then hanging up the paper to dry.

Either way, the solution runs to the bottom so that tabs sold from the bottom of the sheet are stronger than those at the top. The danger is you never know the strength of the LSD tab you have. Even the tiniest amount of LSD will affect the brain, and a large amount could send your brain function over the top and trigger permanent mental illness. *Even touching a tab without gloves could send you on a trip*, so if you find one, beware! LSD deteriorates in sunlight, so old tabs can be dangerous.

Accidents can happen very easily when under the drug's influence. Driving a car or bike or operating machinery is very dangerous indeed.

Although LSD is not physically addictive, it causes *psychological* dependence. After several days of regular use, a user will develop resistance to its effects. The user must then stay off the drug for a while in order to get the same effects again.

The regular user may become deep thinking, with pseudo-religious experiences. However, terrifying hallucinations may occur, with overwhelming feelings of panic and despair. These occur particularly if the user is anxious or depressed, and suicide may be attempted.

Remember all the 'fliers' in the 1960s and 70s when LSD was the 'cool' thing to do? Users thought that they were birds and could fly. These still happen. They simply fall off of tall buildings. Paul dealt with 15 in 28 years as a police officer. The youngest was 11 years old. He had found a tab in big brother's bedroom, and if big brother could do it, so could he!

If LSD is used for some time users can become out of touch with the real world. They remain psychologically disturbed and depressed, particularly if already that way inclined before use. LSD stays in the body for life, and 'flashbacks' (vivid images of a previous trip, good or bad) can occur suddenly at any time. These can be very dangerous and extremely disturbing.

Some Other Drugs

Alcohol
A depressant drug found in wines, spirits and beers.

Alcohol reduces inhibitions and self-control; impairs reactions, judgment, co-ordination and ability to reason. User may feel relaxed and cheerful at first.

There is a danger of accidents, loss of consciousness, and over-dose with a risk of damage to many organs of the body.

It is physically and psychologically addictive.

Barbiturates
These are depressant drugs which can cause physical and psychological dependance. Effects are similar to those of alcohol. There is a great risk of death from overdepressing the breathing mechanism.

Gammahydroxybutyrate (GHB)
Also known as 'GBH' and 'Liquid X', GHB was once used as a pre-operative anaesthetic. It is a colourless liquid, sold in small bottles or by the capful, and has a slightly salty taste. It is a very risky drug to use, as the concentration of the drug is never known. It is a 'downer' in its effects, which are similar to those of alcohol.

It is an illegal drug and is sold mainly to enhance sex, although there is no evidence to prove it does this. It should never be mixed with alcohol.

Ketamine
Also known as 'Vitamin K', 'Special K' or 'K', Ketamine is a disso-ciative anaesthetic. When you use it you don't know who you are, or what you are. In fact, you don't feel anything. You can't move, and look like the 'living dead' with your eyes open. You have grotesquely distorted hallucinations. Even experienced LSD users say they were not prepared for this horrifying experience. Like LSD, it can cause flashbacks of the worst kind, particularly after smoking cannabis, and permanent psychological damage. It comes in tablet or capsule form.

Ketamine is the drug which is usually used to adulterate Ecstasy, which doubles the danger of taking 'E'.

Although Ketamine is controlled by the Medicines Act, it is not strictly illegal to possess it, but most experienced drug users won't touch it ever again!

Magic Mushrooms

Also known as 'mushies', magic mushrooms are an hallucinogenic drug. They can be eaten raw, cooked or brewed to produce a food. Similar in effect to LSD but milder.

There is a danger of bad trips, flashbacks, and poisoning through eating the wrong mushrooms. Can trigger mental problems.

Mescaline

Also known as 'peyote', 'cactus buttons' and 'big chief', mescaline is a hallucinogenic drug derived from the mescal (peyote) cactus. Can be taken as capsules, or in the form of peyote cactus buds, eaten fresh or dried, drunk as tea or ground up and smoked with marijuana. Effects are similar to those of LSD, but mescaline also contains other, strychnine-like chemicals which may cause vomiting, tremors and sweating.

The drug concentrates in the liver rather than the brain, and should never be used by people with impaired liver function.

Combined with alcohol, it is very dangerous. The user can become deranged and violent.

Nitrites (amyl nitrite, butyl nitrite)

Also known as 'poppers' or 'snappers', these drugs are vasodilators, i.e. they increase the flow of blood around the body by relaxing the walls of blood vessels. They are fast acting, giving a rush within 30 seconds but can have many long term effects on health.

The only sign of abuse is a bluish skin discoloration.

Phencyclidine

Also known as 'PCP', 'Angel dust', 'crystal' or 'ozone', phencyclidine is a general anaesthetic and hallucinogenic.

Users may become violent, with dilated pupils, and a numbness to pain, making them difficult to restrain. It can cause permanent derangement, and deaths from suicide by overdosing on the drug are common among heavy users.

Abuse of this drug is not common in Europe.

Solvents

These volatile chemicals are depressants, and they include lighter fuels, aerosols, glues and nail-polish remover. Users inhale them through the mouth.

They give a feeling of drunkeness and reduced inhibitions, and induce dizziness, drowsiness, confusion, sickness, and unco-ordinated movements. Signs of abuse include rashes around nose and mouth.

Dangers are from accidents, convulsions, damage to lungs and heart, kidneys and liver. Death from solvents are due mainly to suffocation, accidents or heart failure. Half of all first-time experimenters end up as casualties.

Steroids

Steroids are stimulant drugs. They can be swallowed as pills or injected. They have no immediate mood-altering effects. In the long term they increase strength, power and endurance, and build up muscles.

There is a danger of increased aggression and sex drive, and liver, heart and kidney damage. Development of breasts and premature balding in men; development of male features, irregular periods, growth of body hair, and deepening of voice in women. Can lead to stunted growth in adolescents.

Tobacco

Contains nicotine, a stimulant drug. Can be chewed or smoked. Psychologically addictive. Causes respiratory diseases, narrowing of the arteries, and various cancers. Also risk to unborn babies during pregnancy.

Tranquillisers (Benzodiazepines)
These depressant drugs, commonly known as 'tranx', are swallowed as pills or capsules, sometimes injected. They have a sedative effect, cause sleepiness, unco-ordinated movements, dulled senses. They are psychologically addictive, have extreme withdrawal symptoms – violent headaches, nausea, convulsions.

General Warnings for Drugs Users

Don't drink alcohol with ANY drug. You never know what you are taking, and whether the two will mix.

Don't mix your drugs.

Don't take more if a drug is taking a long time to take effect. If you take more you could end up with an unpleasant experience if they all start working at once.

Glossary

Addiction	A term that can cover anything from intense habitual cravings for coffee or tobacco, to physical and psychological dependence on more potent agents like heroin.
Analgesic	A substance which relieves pain.
Body salts	See electrolytes.
Dependence	A term that relates to physical or psychological dependance on a substance. Psychological dependence involves intense mental cravings if a drug is unavailable or withdrawn. Physical dependence produces physical withdrawal symptoms if the substance is then not taken. There is a loss of control over intake.
Depressant	A drug which depresses the functions of the brain and other parts of the central nervous system.
Designer drugs	A group of unlicensed drugs whose only purpose is to duplicate the effects of certain illegal drugs of abuse, or to provide even stronger ones. They differ in some minor degree from the original drug, enabling the user and supplier to evade prosecution for dealing in, or possession of, an illegal drug. They are very dangerous because their effects are unpredictable, they are often highly

	potent, and they may contain impurities.
Electrolytes	These are mixtures of various minerals that are always present in body fluids such as blood, urine and sweat, and within the cells of the body. The salts play an important role in regulating water balance, acidity of the blood, conduction of nerve impulses, and muscle contraction. The balance between the various salts can be upset by excessive sweating and the action of some drugs.
Hallucinogen	A drug that causes hallucinations – unreal perceptions of surroundings and objects. Common hallucinogens are LSD, magic mushrooms, and cannabis. Alcohol, in large quantities, can also have this effect.
Narcotic	From the Greek word for numbness or stupor, and once applied to derivatives of the opium poppy. Doctors now use the term narcotic analgesics to refer to opium-derived and synthetic drugs that have pain-relieving properties and other effects like those of morphine.
Neurotransmitter	A chemical released from a nerve ending after receiving an electrical impulse. It may carry a message from one nerve to another so that the electrical impulse passes on, or to a muscle to stimulate contraction, or to a gland to stimulate secretion of a particular hormone.
Poison	A substance that, in relatively small amounts, disrupts the structure and/or function of cells, causing harmful and sometimes fatal effects.
Side Effect	A reaction to a drug that can be explained by the established effects of the drug itself.
Stimulant	A drug which stimulates the central nervous system.
Tolerance	The need to take a higher dosage of a specific drug to maintain the same physical or mental effect.
Toxin	A toxin is a poisonous substance such as a harmful

chemical created by a drug interaction with bodily systems.

Withdrawal symptom

Any symptom caused by abrupt stopping of a drug. These symptoms occur as a result of physical dependence on a drug. Drugs that cause withdrawal symptoms after prolonged use include nicotine and heroin.

Where to get Help

Action for Drug Awareness (ADA)

An organisation we started following Leah's death.

We run a helpline, at present on our home 'phone number, for anyone wishing to discuss a problem, cry, shout, swear, or any other emotion they feel at the time, any time, day or night.

We don't claim to be professional counsellors. Our qualification is that we can empathise with all kinds of inner feelings and worries. The caller can then be put in touch with professional counsellors if they wish.

The address is:

Butterfields Lodge
Butterfields Chase
Latchingdon
Chelmsford
Essex CM3 6LE
Tel./fax: 01621 741098

If your message is picked up on the answerphone, we will ring you back, so leave a number and any instructions.

We also travel anywhere we are asked, if at all possible, to give presentations to schools, colleges, etc. or take part in anything else the organisers of the event feel would further drug awareness and education. We have to ask for travelling expenses, and any donation to ADA is gratefully accepted, but is not a requirement.

Paul Betts: Cert., Ed., NEBSS. Dip. Eq. Ops., Advanced Facilitator.
Janet Betts: R.G.N. (formerly working as an assistant medicinal research chemist.)

National Drug Prevention Alliance (NDPA)

ADA is affiliated to the National Drug Prevention Alliance, which is a network of concerned citizens and prevention professionals who believe that drug-free, healthy lifestyles will protect and enhance society and its stability for present and future generations.

NDPA promotes effective policies, using all means available to its members, including prevention, education, intervention, treatment, and legal processes.

If you would like to know more about the NDPA, get in touch with:

Peter and Ann Stoker,
P.O. Box 594
Slough
SL1 1AA
Tel/fax: 01753 677917

National Association of Registered Door Supervisors & Security Personnel (NARDS SP)

Paul is vice-chairman of the above organisation.

NARDS SP has been established to help local authorities, door supervisors, and security companies set up and maintain training and registration schemes throughout the United Kingdom. With an increase in violence and organised crime in the leisure security industry with its almost non-existent accountability factor, NARDS SP has instigated a computerised national register of security companies, door supervisors, and training companies, and has created, at no cost to local authorities, a training and registration scheme.

NARDS SP has taken the experience of top professionals within the leisure industry, coupled them with the knowledge of highly skilled police trainers, and has devised a training and registration package that not only meets Home Office guidelines but exceeds them in every aspect, giving a more professional and accountable stature to leisure industry personnel.

NARDS SP
Dan Brewington
National Headquarters
Baddow Park
Great Baddow
Essex
Tel: 01245 477293 Fax: 01245 478109
email danielb@nardssp.co.uk

Other Helpful Organisations

ADFAM National
This is the national organisation for the families and friends of drug users.
5th Floor
Epworth House
25 City Road,
London
Tel: 0171 638 3700

Families Anonymous
A self-help support group for parents of drug users, with branches in various parts of the country.
Tel: 0171 498 4680

Re-Solv
The society for the prevention of solvent abuse.
  30a High Street
  Stone
  Staffordshire
  ST15 8AW
  Tel: 01785 817885

Alcohol Abuse

Al-Anon/Alateen
A fellowship of relatives and friends of those who have problems with alcohol. Open 10 am–4pm daily.
  Tel: 0171 403 0888

Alcoholics Anonymous
  Tel: 0345 697555

Drinkline
  Tel: 0171 332 0202 (London only) or 0345 32 0202 (all UK)

Wales

TAFS based at:
  44 Mill Street
  Tonyrefail
  Mid-Glamorgan
  Tel: 01443 671999

The Welsh Office
Can give information on services in Wales.
  Cathays Park
  Cardiff
  CF1 3NQ
  Tel: 01222 825592

Scotland

The Scottish Drugs Forum
Can give information on services in Scotland.
  5th Floor
  Shaftesbury House
  5 Waterloo Street
  Glasgow
  G2 6AY
  Tel: 0141 221 1175

Northern Ireland

Health Promotion Branch, DHSS
Can give information on services in Northern Ireland.
  Upper Newtownards Road
  Belfast
  BT4 3SF
  Tel: 01232 524234

The National Drugs Helpline

Gives free advice about drugs, including personal advice on how to talk to your children about drugs, confidential counselling or information on anything to do with taking drugs. It can tell you about services available in your area, what help they can give, and how people can be referred on to more specialised services, such as hospital clinics or residential rehabilitation programmes.

The lines are open 24 hours a day, every day. Anyone can call, whatever their age or interest in drugs. All calls are free and confidential.
  Tel: 0800 77 66 00

Childline

A free and confidential helpline for children.
    Contact by post:
    Freepost 1111
    London N1 OBR
    Tel: 0800 11 11

Compassionate Friends

An organization for bereaved parents.
    Tel: 0117 953639

The Samaritans

For people who need to talk, the Samaritans provide a listening ear. Their service is manned 24 hours a day.
    National Lo-Call telephone number: 0345 909090 or look in your local telephone directory for your local branch.

Crimestoppers

If you have any information about any crime, phone Crimestoppers on 0800 555 111

·   Your call is free
·   You do not have to give your name
·   You may receive a reward

Drug Smuggling

Help Customs to fight drug smuggling.
    If you notice anything suspicious, dial the Drug Smuggling Action Line.
    Tel: 0800 59 5000

Acknowledgements

It is traditional in books of this kind to have a page set aside for acknowledgements. In this particular case we could easily fill a complete chapter, such has been the huge amount of support and advice we have been fortunate enough to receive.

Almost certainly, if we tried to list each and every person who offered advice or help in any form, someone would be inadvertently omitted, and we are anxious not to cause any offence by overlooking anyone we should have included.

For that reason, we would like to thank our family and friends, for their love and support over what has been a difficult time.

The tragedy of Leah's death has proved beyond doubt what good family and friends we have, and we have also been fortunate to meet many other people, whom we would not normally have encountered, who deserve a mention.

So, here we go. We would like to thank the following individuals:

Sarah Cargill, for her undying love for Leah, for her courage for speaking out, and for her devotion to us.

Andy Hamill, without whose invaluable assistance we would not have been able to cope with the media attention during the four weeks following Leah's death, for arranging our daily timetable during that period, and for his support to William, our son.

The ambulance crew and all the staff at Broomfield Hospital, Chelmsford, for caring for Leah, and Public Relations officers **Peter Laurie** and **Stephanie Martin,** who introduced us to the media.

To the media for being sensitive, truthful, sympathetic and for keeping the debate open and alive to make everyone aware of drug use and abuse.

British Telecom, Richard Madeley and Judy Finnegan, Granada Television and the production team of **Sue Durkan, Jason Nicholls, Mike Marson, Clive Cowan, Robin McDonell, David Attoe** and **Ian McBride,** for their magnificent efforts in both financing and producing the *Sorted* video.

Paul Delaney and his associates for the *Sorted* poster campaign.

Steven Mervish and **Rabbi Saffrin** for setting up our first presentation and for their continued friendship.

The *World in Action* production team of **Sarah Mainwaring-White, George Jesse Turner, Keith Staniforth, Mark Atkinson** and **Duncan Staff** for giving us the knowledge of today's drug culture and the incentive to keep digging.

Paul Foy and **The Society of Vincent de Paul** for their commitment to drug awareness in the Republic of Ireland. We would also like to thank Paul for becoming ADA's Ireland representative! Thanks also for support from the **Eastern Health Board** in Eire.

Joe O'Callaghan and **Cork City Council** and **Pat Duggan** for making all the arrangements for our visits to Cork.

Bob Mills, for putting the humour back into our lives – *'Just like* *that*' – and for becoming ADA's southern England representative.

Ray Hulks and Hampshire Police for their continued support.

NDPA (National Drug Prevention Alliance) for passing on their vision.

Malcolm Grey-Smart and **Alan Adams** for all their prayers.
Essex Police for the professional and compassionate manner in which they dealt with the emergency and for starting off Leah's Appeal with the hefty donation presented to us at Chelmsford Police Station.

The **Metropolitan Police** for raising a substantial amount of money for Leah's Appeal and **Inspector Curtis Parkin** for organizing the events. Also **Peter Shipton** and many other people who helped raise funds for the appeal, whom there are too many to individually mention.

Jason Bartella and the **staff at Pontlands Park Hotel** in Great Baddow, Essex, for their charity evening in aid of Leah's Appeal.

The **Health Education Authority** (and in particular **Andy Seal**) for their invaluable research information.

All the MPs who have taken the issue on board and have taken positive steps against the recreational drugs culture.

Anthea Turner, for showing us that it isn't wrong to ask for donations, and for kissing Paul – three times!

Susan Rees and **Louise, Mike Kelly** and the **management of Secrets nightclub, Romford,** for their fund-raising efforts.

Ronnie Brock, who produced and performed 'We Say No to Drugs' for Leah's Appeal. Thanks also to the schoolchildren who accompanied Ronnie and the management of studio who gave free use of their facilities.

Sony for the permanent loan of a video projector.

NARDS SP (National Association of Registered Door Supervisors and Security Personnel), particularly **Dan Brewington, James Martin** and **Lynwood Newman,** for giving door supervisors respectability and professionalism to help make clubs safer places.

To our dear friends **Don** and **Barbara Gordon** and the **Latchingdon church members** for giving us the strength to carry on – and for encouraging the lamb to return to the fold.

Jackie, 'Sponge', and **the residents of Latchingdon** for use of their club, fund-raising and support.

'Thanks' of a sort to **Sting, Brian Harvey** and **Noel Gallagher** for keeping the debate in the news.

*We want to give **Sue Durkan**, the producer of* Sorted, *a second citation here. She has never received the recognition or praise she deserves for putting* Sorted *on the screen. She will never know just how many youngsters she has touched, giving them a wider and wiser perspective on the drugs issue.*

. . . and to **Ivan, Judy** and **all the family** – what can we say, except Thanks!